essays on
Christianity
and
Political Philosophy

essays on
Christianity
and
Political Philosophy

George W. Carey

James V. Schall, S.J.

editors

UNIVERSITY
PRESS OF
AMERICA

University Press of America

The Intercollegiate Studies Institute, Inc.

Contents

Acknowledgements

These essays were prepared for a Conference on Christianity and Political Philosophy held at Georgetown University, April 18-19, 1980. Acknowledgements and thanks are due to many for the success of this conference and the production of this volume.

The conference was sponsored jointly by the Intercollegiate Studies Institute and the Georgetown University Government Department. Generous support, both moral and material, was also provided by the Dean of the Georgetown Graduate School, the late Donald Hertzberg, by the Provost of the University, Father J. Donald Freeze, S.J., by the Rector of the Jesuit Community, Father James Devereux, S.J., and by Professor Karl Cerny, Chairman, Department of Government. Special appreciation is due to Mr. George Forsyth, previously of the Intercollegiate Studies Institute, presently Editor of the *Claremont Review of Books,* and to Mr. Michael Jackson of the Graduate School at Georgetown University for their assistance and inspiration.

The principal speakers were Professors Gerhart Niemeyer of the University of Notre Dame, Paul Sigmund of Princeton University, Ellis Sandoz of Louisiana State University, the Rev. Clifford Kossel, S.J., of Gonzaga University, and Professor Thomas Molnar of the City University of New York.

Invited as discussants were Professor Elizabeth James of Trinity College, Professor Ross M. Lence of the University of Houston, the late Professor James Steintrager of Wake Forest University, Professor Thomas West of the University of Dallas, and Professor Claes Ryn, Chairman of the Department of Politics at the Catholic University of America.

Robert A. Schadler, formerly Publications Director of the Intercollegiate Studies Institute, Deborah Morrison, and Mary Ehart were especially helpful in the production of this volume.

We are grateful to *Thought,* the Journal of Graduate School, Fordham University, for permission to reprint Professor Ryn's essay and to the late Editor of *Modern Age,* Dr. David S. Collier, for permission to reprint Father Schall's article.

George W. Carey
James V. Schall, S.J.

Christianity and Political Theory:
An Introduction

George W. Carey

THE JUSTIFICATION FOR the conference which prompted these essays is apparent even to those acquainted only with the broad trends in political science. Briefly put, since the middle of this century the discipline of political science, of which political philosophy (theory) is a branch, has been dominated by those of behavioral persuasion. This particular brand of behavioralism, oddly enough, concentrated not so much on how people actually behaved but, rather, on refining the techniques and methods for acquiring data with the end of building a "scientific" political science. This behavioral dominance, in turn, resulted in a shift in "the balance of concern [within political science] from prescription, ethical inquiry, and action to description, explanation, and verification."[1] With this development, political philosophy – and with it the study and analysis of the great classics – assumed a distinctly secondary role in both the undergraduate and graduate curriculums at most institutions.

Given the consequences of what had come to be known as the "behavioral revolution," to say that political theory assumed a secondary role is perhaps an understatement. Today, for instance, only a handful of schools can or do offer a comprehensive doctoral program in political philosophy. Indeed, for many students who received their doctorates after the revolutionary forces had gained ascendancy, Plato, Aristotle, Cicero or Aquinas represent little more than familiar names.

While this, as I have said, is obvious to those with only the slightest familiarity with the trends of the discipline, developments in the late 60s and early 70s served to alter significantly the course of the discipline. This alteration, while seeming to point up the need for a partial restoration of political philosophy to its former status, paradoxically served to diminish its already weakened role. To comprehend and fully appreciate how this remarkable turn of events came to pass, we must understand how many, if not most, behaviorists in the discipline suddenly felt the need to respond to certain inner moral imperatives.

In his presidential address to the American Political Science Association in 1969, Professor David Easton, a leading figure in the behavioral revolution, pointed out what he regarded to be a critical dilemma facing the discipline. "The ideal commitments of behaviorism," he maintained, required a "technical adequacy" without which "the whole evolution of empirical science in all fields of knowledge in the last two thousand years would have been in vain." To achieve and maintain this technical adequacy placed very special demands upon behaviorists. Much like their counterparts in the physical sciences, behaviorists were committed to seemingly endless, painstaking, basic research, even research that often "seems to lead away from the practical, obvious problems of the day." What appear to be "remote, often minute details, about scales, indices, specialized techniques for collecting and analyzing data and the like . . . are the building blocks of the edifice in which more reliable understanding occurs." Easton set forth "the normal ideal commitments of science" in the following terms: "technical proficiency in the search for reliable knowledge, the pursuit of basic understanding with its necessary divorce from practical concerns, and the exclusion of value specification as beyond the competence of science." And these, he believed, represented the "ideals that behavioral research in political science has sought to import into the discipline."[2]

In this same address, however, Easton acknowledged the existence of a mushrooming "post-behavioral" movement—not an "organized" movement but "an aggregate of people" with an "intellectual tendency." The individuals comprising this "inchoate movement" (the "post-behaviorists") did not possess any "special political color" nor did they hold any "particular methodological commitment." They ranged "from conservatism to the active left," from "rigorous scientists" to "dedicated classicists," and their numbers included "all the generations" within the profession.[3]

What were the tenets of this post-behaviorism? Most of them, according to Easton, represented a negative reaction to various aspects of behaviorism. At one level, post-behaviorists had grown disenchanted with the behavioral approach because it embodied "an ideology of empirical conservatism" and "unwittingly purvey[ed] an ideology of social conservatism tempered by modest incremental change." Post-behaviorists accused behaviorists of putting "technique" before "substance," of losing "touch with reality," of shunning their "special obligation to put [their] knowledge to work" to help solve "the struggles of the day." In Easton's words, post-behaviorism "pleads for more relevant research. It pleads for an orientation to the world that will encourage political scientists, even in their professional capacity, to prescribe and to act so as to improve political life according to humane criteria."[4]

Easton felt that it would be ill-advised, if not fatal, for behaviorists to ignore these pleas as "the classicists and traditionalists once did in the face of the onslaught of the behaviorists." The "conditions of the modern world" no longer permit the behaviorists to pursue their researches in splendid isolation. Events, "entirely unpredicted by political science, behavioral or otherwise," have brought about "social crisis" of enormous proportions – e.g., dread of atomic warfare, "mounting internal cleavages in the United States in which civil war and authoritarian rule have become frightening possibilities," and "an undeclared war in Vietnam that violates the moral conscience of the world."[5]

Worse still, Easton argued, "Mankind . . . is working under the pressure of time." The problems are not only grave but urgent; they will not "wait" for the authoritative solutions that only "slow-moving basic research" can provide. Thus, the pleas of the post-behaviorists for greater relevancy in behavioral research, and for the "immediate use" of knowledge, however tentative, relevant to the pressing issues of the day, are thoroughly justified.[6] Indeed, Easton maintained, "For increasing numbers of us it is no longer practical or morally tolerable to stand on the political sidelines when our expertise alerts us to disaster."[7]

These observations led Easton to inquire about why behaviorists failed to anticipate these staggering problems. One answer he set forth is that behaviorists have "not consistently" asked "the question . . . central to the sociology of knowledge: To what extent are our errors, omissions, and interpretations better explained by reference to our normative presuppositions than to ignorance, technical inadequacy, lack of insight, absence of appropriate data, and the like?" Put simply, behaviorists have been wearing blinkers that prevent them from consciously realizing their own "normative presumptions."[8] But this raises the question: "How are [the behaviorists] . . . to break out of the bonds imposed on basic research itself by ongoing value frameworks?" While Easton believed "moral self-scrutiny," an awareness of one's normative presumptions, would certainly help, he saw the need for "returning to an older tradition in a thoroughly modern way." This modern way would borrow a technique employed by "great political theorists of the past," namely, constructing "new and often radically different conceptions of future possible kinds of political relationships." Such undertakings would enable us "to understand better the deficiencies of our own political systems and to explore adequate avenues of change that are so desperately needed." He concluded,

> Both our philosophers and our scientists have failed to reconstruct our value frameworks in any relevant sense and to test them by creatively contemplating new kinds of political systems that might better meet the needs of a post-industrial, cybernetic society. A new set of ethical perspectives woven around this theme might sensitize us to a whole range of new kinds of basic political problems worth investigating.[9]

This "modern way," Easton cautioned, "require[s] boldly speculative theorizing" that would "build upon rather than . . . reject" behavioral findings. As if to suggest that meaningful theoretical inquiries of the future can be undertaken only by those with a firm commitment to the behaviorist credo, he warned: "Those philosophies that seek to revive classical natural law and that reject the possibility of a science of man thereby forfeit their opportunity and put in question their fitness to undertake this creative task of theory."[10]

Whether there is any cause and effect relationship between Easton's proposals and the subsequent trends in political theory need not concern us. It is sufficient to note, for my purposes, that if we read Easton from the perspective of describing and explaining what has occurred, we come up with a fairly accurate picture of the nature and status of political theory in the political science profession today. The new or post-behavioral political theory, oriented towards the goals of behaviorists, is slowly but surely supplanting the more traditional and non-behavioral. It comes as no surprise, then, that Christianity has scarcely any place in the theory curriculum of most institutions. In this regard, Father Schall is quite correct in noting in his essay to follow that a political theory curriculum can be "so designed" and "presented as if Christianity did not exist," precisely because it "is not in practice seen to be connected with the core integrity of the discipline itself."

Moreover, there seems to be no way to bridge the chasm between the approaches and concerns of the "modern way" and those of traditional political theory – a bridging indispensable for the incorporation of any Christian perspectives and contributions into the mainstream of political theory. This is not to say that Christianity is a barren source for creative speculation along lines Easton suggests. On the contrary, as we shall see, it is an excellent source for goals and values quite at variance from those that predominate in the "real world." But these values and goals would not thereby merit any special priorities within the context of the new political theory. Nor, for reasons that will be apparent, would they probably receive anywhere near universal acceptance even among Christians.

We should not conclude from this that Christianity has nothing to contribute to post-behavioral theory. Political theory informed by Christianity certainly possesses the scope and capacity to place the modern trend within the discipline in meaningful perspective. On the other hand, behaviorism can only treat Christianity as a datum, not as the living, vital force it is. We can perceive at least one major reason for the chasm between Christianity and those political theories bent upon serving the ends of behaviorism – to wit, these theories are necessarily based on a shallow and truncated view of man.

These contentions are, I believe, amply illustrated in the following articles by Professors Molnar and Sandoz. Molnar, for instance, shows how the detachment of political theory from Christian political presuppositions antedates Machiavelli, and in what ways the theories of "Ockham, Marsilius, John of Paris, and other radical thinkers of the Middle Ages," have influenced not only church-state relations, but also the nature and authority of civil society as we know it today. According to Molnar, "The emphasis, from the fourteenth to the twentieth century . . . on the separation of Church from State" has resulted in the emergence of State ideology (often totalitarian in character) to fill the vacuum created by "the elimination of the Church as the spiritually and morally ordering principle in State and society." The chasm between Christianity and modern theory would seem to be but a manifestation of the general secular trend Molnar outlines. More significantly, this trend helps to explain, in terms post-behavioral theory cannot, the roots of a major crisis of the modern world – the rejection of moral values and principles that cannot be derived from prevailing secular dogma.

While Sandoz confines himself to a narrower time frame than Molnar, he discovers new dimensions in the American founding period (1761-91) by examining it from the perspectives of classical and Christian thought. Sandoz maintains that "the larger framework of the American vision reached beyond Plymouth and Jamestown, beyond the institutional and theoretical structures of Anglo-American civilization, and even of Western civilization itself as conventionally understood." The Founders realized the "universal reach of their vision," a fact which Sandoz contends accounts for their "sense of exclusiveness and election." Their thought, he continues, "sought its headwaters in the oldest traditions of the civilization and partook in no essential way of the current of radical secularist modernity already swirling around them." These factors, among others, Sandoz believes, account for why it is that "the sobriety of Americans in politics also characterizes their view of history and the nation's destiny."

The conclusions of both Molnar and Sandoz are revealing. More useful here, however, are their approaches, which allow them to deal with the full dimensions of the human experience, including man's quest to know and understand the transcendent and his own place in the order of being. What seems clear is that his knowledge and understanding, no matter how fragmentary, affect in manifold ways the order and direction of societies. In this connection, Professor Niemeyer emphasizes how Christianity, principally through Augustinian theory, served to provide a wider and more meaningful world view than that embraced by the ancients. In Niemeyer's words, "Christian faith provided insights that could not be attained by philosophers on their own, but fitted harmoniously with philosophically-secured truth." Augustine's "concept of history," for example, served to open "the gate for science" and to provide a "meaning and order" for history which was beyond the reach of the ancients. Further, his "double concept of human nature" ("human nature 'as it is from God' " and "human nature 'as vitiated by the sin of defection from God' ") led to an "idea of state" that, according to Niemeyer, ranks as one of the greatest achievements ever in political thought. Since the state embraces both those faithful to God and those motivated by self-love, it is obliged to provide "a peace and order that is commonly good for both of these groupings." Thus, logically, "under no circumstances can the state be a paradigm of perfection, not even in theory."

This Augustinian conception of the state provides us with a framework for better understanding certain recurrent problems surrounding the proper relationship between Christianity and the secular realm of the state, and why, moreover, many contend that certain contemporary Christian doctrines egregiously violate Augustinian prescriptions. Briefly put, the state can be viewed as a "peace treaty" of sorts between those whom, for the sake of convenience, we may call the egotists and the faithful. Though the faithful know they can never write the terms of the treaty to conform fully with their beliefs, goals, and values, they cannot be indifferent to its terms. For the faithful, that is, the treaty should embody the highest common good attainable in this world. But herein lie difficulties and dangers which are explored in the following essays. For instance, Niemeyer considers how to judge the authenticity of claims set forth by the faithful – a problem particularly acute with regard to "Scripture-based political" movements.

Still other questions are these: How extensive and well-defined are Christian teachings that apply to the political realm? What provisions ought the faithful take care to insert into the peace treaty, if possible? Father Kossel's essay is of particular interest in this respect. Aquinas, he notes, "was not a political philosopher, much less a political scientist," and only a small portion of his *Summa* deals directly with the specific concerns of the political community. Nevertheless, certain general teachings do emerge. For instance, though Aquinas seems to be "indifferent" about specific forms of government, he is concerned with "the place and limitations of all human law and societies within the total structure of law and society." The political authority would appear to have an obligation "to care for distributive justice," one that would seem to require regulation of "property, wealth, and social structure to assure all citizens the opportunity to share equitably in the good of the community." Other goals of the political community set forth by Aquinas are similarly general (*e.g.,* "to maintain an order of justice and peace within which men in their associations can carry on their work and growth in reasonable security").

Professor Sigmund emphasizes, however, that there has been in recent times a marked tendency for politically-aware Christians "to identify and justify their political affiliation in religiously-based terms." What is more, these Christians are quite definite about what the provisions of the peace treaty ought to be. But, because these movements have different ideological principles, their provisions differ markedly, often to the extent that they are indistinguishable from those advocated by the egotists. Consequently, serious doubts have arisen whether the Christian view of the state as articulated by Augustine has not broken down entirely. Thus, other questions emerge: Is there really any need today for a peace treaty? Haven't the "worlds" of the egotists and the faithful really merged? Aren't the roles and ends of both politics and religion identical?

Professor Ryn and Father Schall deal with these and like questions in their essays. Their answer, not unexpectedly, is "yes," there has been a definite blurring or merger of politics and religion. Ryn maintains that for many "the old idea that politics at its very best can be found somewhere between divine perfection and gross selfishness would seem too unassuming." The newer and more "ambitious mission of politics must be to establish the rule of love and brotherhood as understood in the teachings of Christ. The Sermon on the Mount and other expressions of the summit of religious aspiration should become the basis for a political program." As a result, politics is invested "with divine potential." In Schall's words, "Rendering to Caesar has become, paradoxically, a clerical occupation, or at least a clerical ambition, as the cynics have always suspected it would."

Both are also adamant that the fusion of the two worlds and the disappearance of the Augustinian framework will have drastic consequences. According to Ryn, "a failure to acquire political prudence and knowledge may lead to endorsement of naive and ultimately destructive proposals." Schall laments that "theology seems presently to state its case before the world precisely in political terms and guises, yet with few of the limits to which political reflection, at its best, is subjected. This makes theology seem more and more unreal, even naive. It often advocates lethal policies in the name of 'justice' without ever even suspecting where political things actually go. . . ."

In short, the fusion of religion and politics in the manner just described places burdens and obligations upon governments that they cannot possibly carry or fulfill. These failures can only produce a sense of frustration and outrage – the more so as one is conditioned to equate failure with injustice. Worse yet, we have seen how these inevitable failures can be attributed, not to the deficiencies of the theories that gave birth to goals impossible to achieve, but rather to those who could not or would not see the "light."

Ryn and Schall would seem correct in pointing out that there must be a delimitation to politics. But any such delimitation cannot possibly originate in the bowels of post-behavioral theory. Quite the contrary. Post-behavioral theory as envisioned by Easton carries with it the dreadful potential of whetting the appetite for the impossible with the confines of a moral vacuum. Nor does classical political thought deal directly and unambiguously with the problem at hand. We should hardly expect otherwise; the problem after all, is the outgrowth of a derailment of Christian teachings.

In my judgment, and this may seem paradoxical, the need for delineation and the form it should assume can only come from Christian thought itself. To maintain this is, of course, to credit Christianity with a unique capacity to come to terms with its derailment within the confines of its own framework. The acute need for the delimitation of politics would not have arisen if more attention had been paid in political philosophy to the relevant and cardinal tenets of Christian doctrine – those tending to produce sobriety and realism concerning man's nature, his malleability, and his potential. The following essays should help determine whether or not this is so.

Notes

[1] David Easton, "The New Revolution in Political Science," *The American Political Science Review* 63 (December, 1969): 1053. This was Professor Easton's Presidential Address to the 65th annual meeting of the American Political Science Association in September, 1969.

[2] *Ibid.*, p. 1054.

[3] *Ibid.*, p. 1051-2.

[4] *Ibid.*, p. 1053.

[5] *Ibid.*

[6] *Ibid.*

[7] *Ibid.*, p. 1060.

[9] *Ibid.*, p. 1057.

[9] *Ibid.*, p. 1058.

[10] *Ibid.*

Reason and Faith:
The Fallacious Antithesis

Gerhart Niemeyer

ALFRED NORTH WHITEHEAD somewhere described evil as "the brute motive force of fragmentary purpose." If one wonders about "purpose," one would hardly go wrong to impute to Whitehead a concept which, like Augustine's concept of will, embraces effect, imagination and memory, with striving. If this be valid, "fragmentary purpose" would be an aspect of "fragmentary reality." The antonym of "fragmentary purpose" we take to be something like "wholeness of purpose," or "wholeness of reality." One is reminded of a similar description of heresy which also centers on the fragmentary kind of heretical belief: "Nearly every heresy is a one-sided and exaggerated expression of some truth. The heretic sees one side of truth very clearly indeed, and refuses to believe that there are other sides. He takes a statement which is symbolic, treats it as if it were a literal fact, and proceeds to build an argument about it, as if he knew all about it."[1]

These remarks are made so that I may enter, at one particular point, into a fragmentary discussion of a huge subject that properly requires treatises merely for the definition of its term: faith and reason. The difficulty of definition is augmented in this essay, as I shall argue, by an antithetical separation of the two, yet one must make a distinction. Do we call reason that which "the human mind, left to itself" spells out to explain to itself the world? Defined that way, the works of the human mind would necessarily include those of the "myth-making faculty," and thus all but the few "higher" religions. It also would include the "natural theology" of the philosophers or philosophical systems, not only Plato and the Stoa, but also Plotinus. Thus it becomes impossible to draw a line between reason and faith along the boundary between the natural and the supernatural. Hence, if we insist on starting out from a sharply antithetical notion of reason vs. faith, we find ourselves compelled to locate it in the positivistic fact-value dichotomy with its initial decision "to do without God," and "to submit to the object." In other words, the antithesis as such is very recent, and very, very young indeed. To reason, defined as "objectivism," faith would necessarily stand opposed as nothing but a subjective "preference." We recognize in these terms a modern jargon signalling to us that we are on familiar but also dangerously treacherous ground.

Instead of making an argument in abstraction, I shall focus this essay primarily on two thinkers, Augustine and Richard Hooker. Augustine is selected because he, first trained in Greek philosophy, and then "by Christ" in Scripture, is the first thinker in whom we can clearly trace what happens when one refuses to say "either-or" and dares say "both-and"; Richard Hooker, because he is the first thinker to recognize, and analyze as "fragmentary," an argument from faith alone that will not stand the test of reason. Augustine's thought can be dubbed "meta-critical," Hooker's "anti-ideological." Both thinkers can be said to achieve a wholeness of "purpose," or of consciousness, in keeping with Whitehead's dictum. Neither is presented here by way of a contribution to specialist studies of these thinkers.

II

A GENERALLY accepted assumption about Augustine is that he was strongly influenced by Neo-Platonism and that he Christianized it as he worked it into his intellectual building. I prefer to take my *point d'appui* with Rudolf Schneider, who in the course of an intensive effort extending over a quarter of a century,[2] has definitively established: (a) that Augustine's entire thought is shot through and through with ontology even though he never established a system of ontology, and (b) that Augustine's ontology is wholly Aristotelian. It seems that Augustine, who of Aristotle's works read only *The Categories,* obtained his knowledge of Aristotelian philosophy in the schools of Carthage, and from his reading of Cicero. At any rate, all of Aristotle's important ontological concepts can be found in Augustine's *de trinitate, de civitate Dei, de genesi ad litteram,* and in his controversy with Julian of Eclanum, not to speak of many other works. Schneider's later book focuses on the soul, a topic in which all important ontological concepts play a key role. Schneider shows that the following conceptual elements of ontology are common to Aristotle and Augustine:

The *analogia entis,* by virtue of which both thinkers distinguish between hierarchical levels of being;

potency and act, by virtue of which both agree that a being having active and passive potency cannot be pure act and thus cannot exist by itself;

the *categories;*

the *transcendental qualities,* for example, the concept of oneness (*unum*) used virtually as a synonym for a being composed of form and matter;

the *inner sense* that apperceives the situation of being, the norm, and the appropriate action;

the *ground* (*aitia*), entering into the ontological structure of the soul as form, end, and movement, and into the general notion of composite beings;

the *soteria tou einai,* which Augustine translates as both *salus* and *esse conservare,* and which we may render as *renewal of being* or *preservation of being* although *salvation of being* would be literal;

the *concept of nature,* comprising the principles of movement, essence, and essence-end-movement.

This list, while not full, suffices as a foil for pointing out Augustine's further developments by means of Scripture.

We shall emphasize here chiefly the differences between Augustine's and Aristotle's anthropology and theology, always keeping in mind the basic concepts shared between the two. Aristotle's anthropology centers on the insight that man, composed of body and soul, form and matter, depends on other beings for the renewal and preservation of his being. He needs food to sustain the growth of his form, and, after completion of the growth, to sustain the continued existence of the developed form. Thus in order to be happy, man requires external goods as well as goods of the body. As he also needs goods of the soul, he is dependent on the fellowship with other human beings to enjoy them. Still, Aristotle

is aware that the combination of form and matter cannot be
secured indefinitely. While the form is the ruling element, matter
retains a certain autonomy by virtue of which it outlasts the
destruction of the form. Hence man, to save his being, must rely on
procreation, saving human beings through the species. Also man
requires for his well-being a political association so that he may attain to the "good life" in which rulers and ruled combined seek to
save their being in association. To his gnawing concern with man's
propensity to destruction, Aristotle provides two ultimate
answers: (a) in a virtuous political order which fully develops the
potency of the human soul, in company with others, man can attain
what Aristotle calls "self-sufficiency," *i.e.* a deliverance from his
ontic precariousness; and (b) even beyond this, man, striving to
"immortalize," may lift his mind to the contemplation of the *aitia*,
the eternal things, in pure *theoria*, in which his human concerns
with external goods and goods of the body recede in importance, so
that the threat of changes and misfortunes seems forgotten. These
two constitute Aristotle's attempt to find "solutions" to the problem of man's ontic instability and dependence, solutions that seem
to lie within human powers of attainment.

At this point Augustine carries Aristotle's ontological insights
consistently further, beyond Aristotle's psychological conclusions
and practical remedies. He does this by introducing the concept of
man's "mutable" being, mutable as contrasted with the *actus purus*
of God. "Mutability" means, on the one hand, that man is the one
created being that also can conduct itself so as to change its nature
for the worse. Thus, where Aristotle sees mainly the propensity of
circumstances to changes, and the likely turns of "fortune's wheel,"
Augustine sees human life more profoundly insecure than that. To
use the modern words of Romano Guardini instead of Augustine's:
" . . . the existing order of things, indeed of life itself seems but
loosely, precariously balanced across the chaos of existence and its
uncontrollable forces. All rules seem temporary, and threaten to
give way at any moment. Things themselves appear now shadowy,
now ominous. Reality is by no means as substantial as it may seem,
and personal existence, like all existence, is surrounded by and
suspended over the powerful and perilous void. . . ."[3] With all his
closeness to Aristotelian categories and conceptual structures,
Augustine draws from them a view that is worlds beyond the sunlit
cosmos of the Stagirite. Sharing Aristotle's insight that the

renewal and preservation of being entail dependence on other beings (things and creatures), Augustine translates this into a
general law of created being (*"esse cum"*) and logically extends it to
essential dependence on the immutable being of God. It follows
that, speaking ontologically, the *salus*, the salvation of man's
precarious being, ultimately cannot be attained in this world of
mutability. Aristotle's "self-sufficiency" can be realized not in the
polis, but only in a new life of union with God. Likewise, Augustine
replaces Aristotle's contemplation (*theoria*), the forgetting of life's
care over the vision of the *aitia*, with man's *peregrinatio*, his
pilgrimage to God. This implies more than a shift from a solution in
the mind to a solution in the whole of life. It also means a shift from
a static to an historical and dynamic principle.

> Yet those doubtless judge better who prefer to that knowledge the
> knowledge of themselves: and that mind is more praiseworthy which
> knows even its own weakness. . .for he has preferred knowledge to
> knowledge, he has preferred to know his own weakness, rather than
> to know the walls of the world, the foundations of the earth, and the
> pinnacles of heaven. And by obtaining this knowledge, he has
> obtained also sorrow (*dolor*); but sorrow for straying away from the
> desire of reaching his own proper country, and the Creator of it. . . .
> Visions have been sent to us from heaven suitable to our state of
> pilgrimage, in order to remind us that what we seek is not here, but
> that from this pilgrimage we must return thither, whence unless we
> originated we should not here seek these things."[4]

Augustine does not discard the treasure of Aristotle's contemplation, but realizes that pure contemplation will begin only at the end
of that pilgrimage, where being is ultimately delivered from any
threat of nothingness. Here roots Augustine's psychology, here his
concept of will prominently involving the affects, memory and imagination, here also roots ultimately his Christology, all ontologically founded. "Augustine has established the prevalence of
ontology in Christian theology!"[5]

Theology is Augustine's other great improvement over Aristotle.
Both Plato and Aristotle, and not only they but Stoics and Neo-
Platonists as well, had developed a more or less philosophical
(natural) theology. Aristotle's was confined to a few bare outlines.
His God is *actus purus* and thus self-subsistent, and prime origin of
all movement. Plato, Aristotle's teacher, had known more. He had

more than once given profound and convincing accounts of noetical, mystical experiences of the Beyond. Apart from psychology, however, Aristotle's God is even ontologically inadequate. "Aristotle does not see that, when he understands God as a being existing in himself, everything outside God must in its existence and essence depend on God, if the concept of God is not to be made meaningless."[6] That leads to the following appraisal of Augustine as compared with Aristotle: "Aristotle has failed to carry through his ontological insights in the other disciplines, systematically and consistently. Augustine has proceeded much more systematically and consistently."[7] The reason for Augustine's greater power of unity and principle lies in his biblical faith. That faith, of course, did not come to him as the fruit of analysis and contemplation. All the same, he accepted it and committed himself on the ground of reasonableness as well as authority.

Thus Augustine's conversion must have had not only that deeply liberating personal effect of which he tells us in the *Confessions,* but also the effect of supplying for his philosophy "the other half," hitherto missing. Beginning with Aristotle's prime mover, he now sees further that God is creator of everything, the origin of all existence because he *is* existence itself, the maker of all essences, a good God whose created things are all good, a God who annihilates nothing but cares for, and saves, being. Thus to the total ancient philosophy, Augustine adds (a) the personal God, (b) the goodness of God and of all created natures, (c) the Christian faith in the recovery of the original goodness of creation by grace, beyond temporal-spatial existence. Further, Augustine had learned through his own experience "that the situation of being, the *unum,* must first be changed if one is to attain to the knowledge of the *verum.* Augustine's great achievement in ontology is his insight that the oneness of being has primacy before knowledge and will – an insight which in general theory was already available before him."[8]

Even though Augustine boasts that he was "taught by Christ and not by Aristotle and Chrysippus," he has no practical difficulty with assimilating one to the other. Christian faith provided insights that could not be attained by philosophers on their own, but fitted harmoniously with philosophically secured truth. Mortimer Adler has said: "Philosophy produces a shell into which faith can be poured." It may be more accurate that philosophy provides a structure in which faith finds confirmation of its reasonableness, in turn providing that structure with depth and height in which consciousness attains wholeness. Whitehead's wholeness of purpose certainly must include concern with vision of eternal things capable of overcoming man's exclusive preoccupation with short-range temporal purposes. The problem of faith and reason, however, is not located at this point. The problem is found in the way in which the philosopher arrives at the idea of God by way of inferring strong probabilities from his observation of things seen and unseen. "There *must be* . . ." is what he says. There must be a prime mover, an ultimate One, a workman-creator, a divinity *beyond* the gods of our fathers, and so on. God is a product of philosophic intuitive speculation. This is essentially belief. Belief also figures in religion, but religion moves beyond belief to commitment, reliance, trust, and submission. Thus Augustine, in filling his works with scriptural quotations (even though his thought merged them with philosophical structure) created for his readers the difficulty that they could not accept the authority of Scripture except by a "leap of faith," a personal risk which to them might appear a betrayal of reason. Reason was taken for something all men had in common, but faith as something common only to those who had personally committed themselves, and thus as something "subjective." Augustine himself made clear that "praise of God" is a requirement for that kind of knowledge which he had added to ancient philosophy. Faith and love, thanksgiving and praise, are personal as well as corporate acts, which, to those who for some reason will not or cannot join, appear as illegitimate intruders in the impersonal universe of philosophical reasoning, and present a false note in the philosophical ideal of practical life according to Aristotle's formula, "deliberation without passion." Reason versus faith, then, is a conflict not between two varieties of belief, but rather between an intelligible universe that opens up only as an individual submits to it with praise and thanksgiving, and one whose access risks no more than the acceptance of its axioms.

Two remarks can be made about this. The first rests on the findings of a modern book, that the supposed risklessness of philosophical and scientific thinking is an illusion, an illusion erected into a dogma by "objectivism" in our modern age.[9] Polanyi proves in countless ways that there is no such thing as the impersonal action of the object on the human mind, so that "objectivism" itself is a belief, and an unreasonable one at that. Rather, says Polanyi, all knowledge involves an element of intellectual passion, a tacit component of previous beliefs, as well as a personal commitment.

> Like the tool, the sign or the symbol can be conceived as such only in the eyes of a person who *relies on them* to achieve or signify something. *This reliance is a personal commitment which is involved in all acts of intelligence by which we integrate some things subsidiarily to the centre of our focal attention.* Every act of personal assimilation by which we make a thing form an extension of ourselves through our subsidiary awareness of it, is a commitment of ourselves. . . .[10]

This "personal" element, however, must not be confused with "subjectivism":

> . . . personal knowledge in science is not made but discovered, and as such claims to establish contact with reality beyond the clues on which it relies. It commits us, passionately and far beyond our comprehension, to a vision of reality. Of this responsibility we cannot divest ourselves by setting up objective criteria of verifiability – or falsifiability, or testability, or what you will. For we live in it as in the garment of our own skin. Like love, to which it is akin, this commitment is a 'shirt of flame,' blazing with passion, and, also like love, consumed by a devotion to a universal demand.[11]

> . . . this personal coefficient, which shapes all factual knowledge, bridges in doing so the disjunction between subjectivity and objectivity.[12]

For myself, I wish that Polanyi had chosen another term in lieu of "passion." Henri Bergson, philosophizing in a similar vein, points to "emotion" as the source of all creation. Augustine's wide-spanning concept of "love" comes to mind; and a modern writer might well speak of "the affects." All these amount to what Polanyi means. Going beyond a mere analysis of the process of knowledge, Polanyi severely criticizes "the principle of moral and religious indifference which prevails throughout modern science"[13] and insists "that science can then no longer hope to survive on an island of positive facts, around which the rest of man's intellectual heritage sinks to the status of subjective emotionalism."[14]

The other remark must question the subjectivism attributed to Augustine by those who find his Scriptural dependence one which is invalid because they cannot personally share it. "Augustine," says Rudolf Schneider, "does not insist exclusively on the world of his own experiences, but believes firmly in the existence of real, external being beyond all experiences. Because there is being, there can be experience. Because there is reality, there can be subjectiveness. . . ."[15] To put it differently, Augustine believes in, and speaks of, the same reality as the philosophers. He might have invoked Bergson's distinction between the knowledge "of the object . . . a knowledge attained by the intellect . . . that is sought for its utility to man, and which enables him to manipulate matter, and thereby, to control it and act upon it," and "absolute knowledge" which does not "move around its object but enters into it" and which "attains the absolute" but, in order to do so, must be "in sympathy with reality without any thought of relation or comparison." Thus reality has dimensions into which one must enter with faith, praise, and worship if one is to understand at all. "Believe that you may understand; understand that you may believe."[16] There are dimensions of reality which must remain not only unintelligible but even unimaginable to the closed soul. The open soul, however, loving and praising, while disciplined in virtue, will attain a width of vision in which its knowledge of objects is not denied but finally placed in the fullness of context.

On the other hand, nobody can deny that Augustine's *Confessions* is a most subjective work. It has been called the first autobiography – wrongly, I believe, for the modern autobiography, on the model of Rousseau, penetrates into the self in isolation from the world, indeed, in hostility against all that exists. By contrast, in his *Confessions,* Augustine "describes the mutation of his subjectivity to God."[17] The proof is that he, through divine grace, rediscovered an interest in the things of this world. "The path to this point goes through the awareness and experience of the fallibility of external things and of virtue. Along this path the interest in things is diminished until it is completely destroyed by despair so that there is left only the knowledge of the hopeless *infirmitas.* Through grace a new interest in things is kindled and they are seen in the way in which they are from God. The relation of God as *actus purus* to the mutable world becomes the central theme and the new vision of man renewed by grace."[18] One must distinguish here between the personal elements of religion and its public aspects. Augustine has portrayed his personal conversion and salvation. What he communicated publicly, however, was the *doctrina christiana,* which results in general assumptions commonly held, entering into any human endeavor and awareness. This is what one may call Christian culture, a pattern largely independent of personal religious events, even though such events continuously feed and develop it. Christian culture is not the same as the Church. The Church, in turn, exists as a public community of praise and worship, of faith and love, independent of whether every single one of its members is or is not a believing Christian. In the same way, Christian culture will long survive the Christian convictions of individual members. Its basic assumptions will continue to govern much of human thinking, feeling, knowing and acting even when Christianity itself, within the culture, may have come under severe attack and, indeed, disdain.

One must expect, then, that Augustine's ability to penetrate, with the love of the open soul, into aspects of reality barred to the critically closed soul, would bring about a net increase of rationality in the total world view. Let us corroborate this expectation by means of three samples: Augustine's view of human nature, his concept of history, and his idea of the state.

III

SINCE PLATO AND ARISTOTLE, the concept of nature, and especially that of human nature, has provided the chief norm for the order of human life. Essence was taken as the ultimate ground of inner possibility, so that man's essence rules his movement, *i.e.,* his coming-to-be what he is. Reliance on nature as norm, however, led Plato to remark that a city in accordance with human nature was not to be found on earth, but was laid up in heaven; while Aristotle despaired of finding a city with a hundred fully developed, mature men (*spoudaioi*) in it. Both Plato and Aristotle (the former in *The Laws,* the latter in Books IV-VI of *Politics*) were compelled to speak of order in the midst of perversion, where nature appeared as a concept of scant relevance. Augustine, by contrast, developed two concepts of human nature. The first describes human nature "as it is from God," good in the proportion and hierarchical order of all its parts, and meant to cleave to God for the security of its being. The second concept is that of human nature as vitiated by the sin of defection from God. Augustine saw man as the only creature capable of changing its nature, or rather, corrupting it, which would not be possible if its nature were not originally good. The result is a perverted nature, subject to inferior forces, bad habits, and inner disunity. Fallen man is endemically disobedient not only to God, but also to himself. The vitiated nature, however, still has the endurance of a form, albeit a form defective in its false loves and bad dispositions. Augustine's two concepts enable him to account for the irrationalities of social and political life on this earth, for the "discontents" besetting all civilization. He can also refer the problem of inescapable failure of even our best efforts to the perfection awaiting those who cleave to God, without thereby committing himself to a gnostic declaration of war on the world of created things around us.

Augustine's concept of history was perhaps his most incisive break with ancient philosophy and culture. He perceived "the contingency of the universe" and thereby opened the gate for science.[19] For the ancients, who looked to nature for final ends, history was without meaning or order. On the other hand, they considered the future predictable, since augury and oracle contained keys to its knowledge. Men relying on this knowledge, however, again and again found themselves misled, so that precisely where they looked for certainty, they reaped a besetting insecurity. *Tyche* and *Fortuna* were powerful deities, but also notoriously capricious. Man's well-being in this world was subject to radical and lightning-fast turns of "the wheel of history." Worse yet, the quest for the "good state" or "the best state" seemed almost quixotic. In the words of Frederick D. Wilhelmsen:

> Given a polity firmly based on an understanding of the structure of reality; given a compact nucleus of virtuous men heading this society and governing it according to good laws; given the ideal of virtue as a public goal acting as a leaven throughout the whole community making good men better, indifferent men good, and bad men ashamed; given the material power and technology necessary to maintain itself against all internal and external enemies; given a level of civilization incomparably superior to that of the rest of the world; given all these things, and then add to them failure, not a failure unforeseen but one first adumbrated as the most remote and trivial of possibilities and later sensed as a real menace which ought to be rejected as absurd

and even indecent, and then add again a failure now accepted as an
inevitable fatality whose sentence of death can only be postponed by
rear guard tactics; given all this, and we are given a polity confronted
crudely and inexorably with the powers of unintelligibility, the vacant
stare of the absurd.[20]

This is a conclusion which Marcus Tullius Cicero, falling under
the murderer's steel, had to acknowledge with his last breath. It
also would have been the conclusion to which Rome's sack by the
barbarians, in 410, would have driven a pagan philosopher. For
Augustine, however, the death of Jesus Christ on the cross, and his
resurrection to eternal life, were the great light planted at the very
center of apparent absurdity. Moved by his faith in the revealed
meaning of God's death, Augustine could see history as the great
movement from the corruption of man's being to its ultimate salvation, to man's deification in union with God. This also made possible
a concept of Providence, the humanly unknowable but purposeful
dispositions of a good creator and redeemer God. History's im-
penetrable irrationality thus vanished. A new sense of freedom
resulted. "The stars, in their unalterable courses, did not, after all,
implacably control our destinies. Man, every man, no matter who,
had a direct link with the Creator, the Ruler of the stars
themselves. . . . It was no longer a small and select company which,
thanks to some secret means of escape, could break the charmed
circle: it was mankind as a whole which found its night suddenly il-
luminated. . . . No more circle! No more blind hazard! No more
Fate! Transcendent God, God the friend of men, revealed in Jesus,
opened for all a way which nothing would ever bar again."[21] The
future, once considered predictable by magic and deceptive means,
now appeared open, its possibilities a human responsibility, its
ultimate outcome in the hands of a God of Love. "The future is
open, and it is God's." Nor was any speculation on the basis of a
scriptural numbers game allowed to take the place of faith and
Christian patience. The whole of history is intelligible because it
moves toward an ultimate eschatological goal of divine justice and
fulfillment.

Augustine's idea of the state ranks with his double concept of
human nature as one of the greatest achievements ever in political
thought. A radical Christian other-worldliness would have echoed
Tertullian's view: "Thus there is nothing more alien to us than

public affairs." A superficial reading may suggest that this was also Augustine's view. For he distinguished between two principles of human association: ". . . two cities have been formed by two loves: the earthly by the love of self, even to the contempt of God; the heavenly by the love of God, even to the contempt of self. The former, in a word, glories in itself, the latter in the Lord." The earthly city is not identical with the state, however, nor the heavenly with the Church. They are what in modern jargon are called "lifestyles," diametrically opposed. Their mutual exclusiveness, however, does not spell civil war. The state is instituted to keep a peace and an order that is commonly good for both of these groupings. The state, then, is homogeneous neither in religious nor in moral terms. The faithful of God cannot dictate terms of highest virtue, nor can the mass of egotists write their vices into law. This means that under no circumstances can the state be a paradigm of perfection, not even in theory.

On the other hand, it cannot be considered a matter of indifference by Christians. As a framework of peace, it constitutes the highest common good "on this earth." As composite as each individual person, the state has no power to exist in itself. It remains beset by tendencies toward failure and nothingness. But even in the wretchedness of "alienation from God," Augustine finds the possibility of "peace," *i.e.,* order and justice. Just as human nature, vitiated by sin, still manifests an order, even in perversion, so the state, populated by good and evil at the same time, operates under a law of order which Augustine spells out in the great chapters 12-17, and 24, of Book XIX of the *City of God.* Substituting for Cicero's unduly idealizing concept of a people ("an assembly of rational beings where concepts of true justice are acknowledged") a better, because it is a more empirical, concept ("an assemblage of reasonable beings bound together by a common agreement on the objects of their love"), Augustine likewise moves the concept of the state to the ground of realism. The state, in keeping peace and order, is the most important worldly institution in which all Christians should fully cooperate. Not being born from a community of the highest virtues nor even from one of the highest aspirations, the state, in keeping peace and order, is not performing a task of salvation. The highest destiny of man lies beyond the state, because it cannot be attained in space or time, or even by human powers alone. It will come by God's grace, beyond history and death. In his political theory, then, Augustine is not writing with the pen of theology. Cast in wholly ontological terms which are adapted to this-worldly realism by introducing the concept of original sin, Augustine's political order speaks to all, believers and non-believers alike. Realizing that the state, comprising within itself morally mixed company, can never amount to human perfection, Augustine has created the concept of the *limited* state, which has remained a hallmark of Western civilization.

IV

AUGUSTINE WAS the first philosopher to succeed in combining knowledge attained by virtue of faith in revelation with knowledge attained by the critical discipline of philosophical intellect. Even though critical philosophy as we know it came into existence only in modern times, one may well call Augustine the first post-critical thinker, who methodically and deliberately explored the relation between faith and reason in the wholeness of consciousness. If we now turn to Richard Hooker, we do so because we find in him another kind of discovery regarding that relation. His writing was prompted by finding in the 16th century English Puritans (and their *"Admonition of Parliament"* of 1572) a kind of consciousness that was feeding on faith while disregarding or even abandoning the bond of reason. It was Hooker's achievement to have recognized and analyzed this as a type of "fragmentary consciousness," awareness which should have come, but did not, from the authorities of the Church of England. Hooker, a relatively obscure priest, wrote *The Laws of Ecclesiastical Polity* "though for no other cause but for this; that posterity may know we have not loosely through silence permitted things to pass away as in a dream. . . " – surely one of the most memorable opening sentences of any book. The Puritans' *Admonition* had demanded that the laws of England, particularly those pertaining to the Established Church, should be replaced by laws exclusively derived from the Bible, selected by Calvinist interpretation.

In his *Preface,* Hooker directly addresses the Puritans: "Surely the present form of church-government which the laws of this land have established is such, as *no law of God nor reason of man* hath hitherto been alleged of force sufficient to prove they do ill, who to the uttermost of their power withstand the alteration thereof" (emphasis supplied). Contrariwise: "The other, which instead of it we are required to accept, is only by error and misconceit named the ordinance of Jesus Christ, no one proof as yet brought forth whereby it may clearly appear to be so in very deed."[22] Hooker's criticism from the first invokes his own belief: ". . . there are but two ways whereby the Spirit leadeth men into all truth; the one extraordinary, the other common; the one belonging but unto some few, the other extending itself unto all that are of God; the one, that which we call by a special divine excellency Revelation, the other Reason."[23]

The Puritans held their belief not in conjunction with their reason, but separate from it, so that they adamantly refused to enter into any discursive "conference." This led Hooker to probe for the defects of such a consciousness – defects he located through the following symptoms: (a) self-justification ("a singular goodness") based indirectly on the radical nature of their total critique of England's ecclesiastical order; (b) tracing all the world's evil to the extant institutions of ecclesiastical government; (c) asserting that the proposed Puritan institutions will be "the sovereign remedy of all evils"; (d) a reductionism that finds in Scripture only evidence supporting the Puritan demands; (e) the resulting "high terms of separation between such and the rest of the world." In his own summary of this attack, Hooker attributes to the Puritans: "A custom of inuring your ears with reproof of faults especially in your governors; an use to attribute those faults to the kind of spiritual regiment under which you live; boldness in warranting the force of their discipline for the cure of all such evils; a slight of framing your conceits to imagine that Scripture every where favoureth that discipline; persuasion that the cause why ye find it in Scripture is a seal unto you of your nearness of God."[24] He accuses the Puritans of having formed "a cause," using the term precisely as we do to-day, when speaking of someone as *"engagé."* The "cause" is a world apart, not merely distinct from the world in which all men live together, but antithetical to it, and thus claiming for itself a singular, indeed, an ontic merit compared with which the rest of the world appears as mere refuse. The members of "the cause" are distinguished by a special knowledge that stems from their "nearness to the Spirit," or the possession of Marxism-Leninism – to whatever source of truth from which all others are barred. Such faith is neither proclaimed to others with a view to sharing it, nor defended by argument. It is used as a title of certainty about which one cannot communicate, and which admits between "the cause" and the rest of men only the relation of conquest and submission.

This led Hooker to reflect deeply on the relation between faith and reason. "The general and perpetual voice of men is as the sentence of God himself. For that which all men have at all times learned, Nature herself must needs have taught; and God being the author of Nature, her voice is but his instrument."[25] In a sentence that recalls the famous dictum of the great Muslim mystic, Ghazali, "reason is God's scale on earth," Hooker states, "Wherefore the natural measure whereby to judge our doings, is the sentence of Reason determining and setting down what is good to be done."[26] And, with reference to the laws of ecclesiastical policy, he remarks: ". . . those Laws are investigable by Reason, without the help of Revelation supernatural and divine."[27] Finally, Hooker's teaching is thus summed up: "It sufficeth therefore that Nature and Scripture do serve in such full sort, that they both jointly and not severally either of them be so complete, that unto everlasting felicity we need not the knowledge of any thing more than these two may easily furnish our minds with on all sides. . . ."[28] The general idea can already be found in Thomas Aquinas. Hooker's specific achievement is the analysis of a Scripture-based political movement as one whose pretended godliness is spurious because its message denies and evades the common bond of reason that is valid for the relations of men with men. In a somewhat similar vein, the Muslim mystic Quchairi, speaking on the subject of "intuitions," states that they may come from angels, Satan, the natural man, or from God himself. "These," he says, "can be recognized in the following way: an intuition from an angel will be in conformity with reason and will lead to good works; an intuition from Satan will lead to sin, while an intuition from Nature will lead one to follow one's natural propensities, particularly pride and lust. . . ."[29]

V

IT SHOULD BE CLEAR by now that we have not attempted anything general about the topic of faith and reason, but have touched only on two particular points suggested by Whitehead's concept of "fragmentary purpose." Purpose, which flows from imagery, memory, love, and striving, can be fragmentary in terms of a reality that is nothing but natural. The central thesis of Michael Polanyi's book, *Personal Knowledge,* is that there is no such thing as a purely "objectivist" science, and that fanatical adherence to that fallacious concept can only destroy science. "The science of today," he says,

> serves as a heuristic guide for its own further development. It conveys a conception about the nature of things which suggests to the enquiring mind an inexhaustible range of surmises. The experience of Columbus, who so fatefully misjudged his own discovery, is inherent to some extent in all discovery. . . . .An empirical statement is true to the extent to which it reveals an aspect of reality, a reality largely hidden to us, and *existing therefore independently of our knowing it.* By trying to say something that is true about a reality believed to be existing independently of our knowing it, all assertions of fact necessarily carry universal intent. . . . .The enquiring scientist's intimations of a hidden reality are personal. They are his own beliefs which – owing to his originality – as yet he alone holds. Yet they are not a subjective state of mind, but convictions held with universal intent, and heavy with arduous projects. . . . .He has reached responsible beliefs, born of necessity, and not changeable at will. In a heuristic commitment, affirmation, surrender and legislation are fused into a single thought, bearing on a hidden reality.[30]

This result, which Polanyi reached through a number of distinct partial analyses, finally enables him to group "the conception of religious worship as a heuristic vision and align religion in turn also with the great intellectual systems, such as mathematics, fiction and the fine arts, which are validated by becoming happy dwelling places of the human mind."[31] And finally:

> The enquiry into the nature and justification of personal knowledge . . . has led to the acceptance of our calling – for which we are not responsible – as a condition for the exercise of a responsible judgment with universal intent. . . . .Calling; personal judgment involving responsibility; self-compulsion and independence of conscience; universal standards; all these were shown to exist only in their relation to each other within a commitment. They dissolve if looked upon non-committedly. We may call this the ontology of commitment. . .
> The paradox of self-set standards and the solution of this paradox are thus generalized to include the standards which we set ourselves in appraising other organisms and attribute to them as proper to them.

We may say that this generalization of the universal pole of commitment acknowledges the whole range of being which we attribute to
organisms at ascending levels.[32]

Augustine's reality was less fragmentary than that of ancient
philosophy because it took in "the whole range of being which we
attribute to organisms at ascending levels." It also turned out to be
a heuristic vision of the most productive kind which, among other
things, produced a rational concept of the whole of history of which
no previous thinker had been capable. The close linkage of faith and
reason, even though the one is acritical and the other critical, turns
out to be ontologically founded rather than being merely a pious
wish to include everything. Hooker taught us the sober alertness
required to hold these two dimensions in the necessary balance and
mutual tension of consciousness. Their linkage can be immensely
productive but contains also destructive potentialities. Where faith
is mistaken for critical knowledge, and critical knowledge allowed
to play the part of faith, a fall into an abyss of inhumanity may
result. Occurrences of this kind are too numerous in our memory to
make the above finding with a sense of triumphant comfort. The
radical "scientist" objectivism that has crippled modernity comes
from a deep fear with which one can sympathize, although emotional sympathy must not be allowed to seduce us into a
philosophical endorsement. We find, once again, that being human
is a risky business, beset on all sides with insecurities and pitfalls.
Vigilance is the price not only of freedom, but also of truth and
"responsible" personal commitment.

Notes

[1] Claude B. Moss, *The Christian Faith* (London: S.P.C.K., 1965), p. 48 f.
[2] Rudolf Schneider, *Das wandelbare Sein* (Frankfurt: Klostermann, 1938);
idem, Seele und Sein, Ontologie bei Augustin und Aristoteles (Stuttgart:
Kohlhammer, 1957).
[3] Romano Guardini, *Meditations before Mass* (Westminster, Md.: Newman
Press, 1955), p. 192.
[4] St. Augustine, *De Trinitate* IV. 1-2.
[5] Schneider, *Seele und Sein,* p. 31.

[6] *Ibid.*, p. 30.

[7] *Ibid.*, p. 31.

[8] *Ibid.*, p. 21.

[9] Michael Polanyi, *Personal Knowledge* (Chicago: University of Chicago Press, 1962).

[10] *Ibid.*, p. 61.

[11] *Ibid.*, p. 64.

[12] *Ibid.*, p. 17.

[13] *Ibid.*, p. 153.

[14] *Ibid.*, p. 134.

[15] Schneider, *op. cit.*, p. 27.

[16] Augustine, *Sermo* 43. 7. 9; 118. 1.

[17] Schneider, *loc. cit.*, p. 20.

[18] *Ibid.*, p. 48.

[19] Stanley L. Jaki characteristically uses this expression in his books and lectures to distinguish a universe that has issued from divine creation and thus might not have been from a universe that is supposed to exist in timeless necessity.

[20] Frederick D. Wilhelmsen, *Christianity and Political Philosophy* (Athens, Ga.: University of Georgia Press, 1978), p. 67.

[21] Henri de Lubac, *The Drama of Atheist Humanism* (Cleveland and New York: Meridian Books, 1963), p. 5.

[22] John Keble, ed., *The Works of Mr. Richard Hooker*, 3 vols. (Oxford: Oxford University Press, 1874), Preface ii. 1.

[23] *Ibid.*, Preface iii. 10.

[24] *Ibid.*, Preface iii. 16.

[25] *Ibid.*, Book I. viii. 3.

[26] *Ibid.*, Book I. viii. 8.

[27] *Ibid.*, Book I. viii. 9.

[28] *Ibid.*, Book I. xiv. 5.

[29] Quoted in R.C. Zaehner, *Mysticism Sacred and Profane* (Oxford: Oxford University Press, 1967), p. 144.

[30] Polanyi, *op. cit.*, p. 311.

[31] *Ibid.*, p. 280.

[32] *Ibid.*, p. 379.

Some Limits of Politics

Clifford Kossel, S.J.

THOMAS AQUINAS WAS not a political philosopher, much less a political scientist. His investigations and thoughts were those of a Christian theologian, a man of faith seeking understanding. As such he focused on human disciplines such as metaphysics, philosophical anthropology, and ethics which could help make manifest anything about God, or the relation of the world, especially of man, to God.[1] Consequently, we find no treatise in his *Summa Theologica* devoted thematically to a philosophy or theology of society, community or state.

This is not to say that he does not deal with these matters. On the contrary, as the treatise of law (I-II) makes abundantly clear, they are integral to his broader concerns. If, as Aquinas would have it, law is the operative organization of a community to achieve its common good, two questions naturally arise: What is a community? What constitutes the common good? Thus, in this treatise, the political community is systematically located, put in its place, and thereby provided with its essential purposes and limitations.

In q. 91, after three articles devoted to eternal, natural, and human law, Aquinas asks in article 4: Why is there need of a divine law (a law explicitly revealed by God)? Why are not eternal, natural, and human laws sufficient for the guidance of human activity? In this article, he explicitly treats four limitations of human law, and, therefore, of political community. (Two of these also apply to natural law.) This article is also a clue to the meaning of the treatise on law. That treatise does not end with q. 97; there are eleven more questions devoted precisely to the divine law, Old and New. Questions 90-97 (which are usually excerpted for paperback editions or anthologies as Aquinas's *Treatise on Law*) are merely a preparation (mostly philosophical) for a better elucidation of the divine law.

The problem may best be seen by starting with I-II:90,1. Having shown that law consists of certain universal propositions of practical reason regulating human activity for some end, Aquinas now asks about that end. Is all law directed to the common good? He answers: Practical reason is the first principle of all human activity. But in reason itself there is something which is the principle of all the rest; this is the ultimate end, which is happiness or beatitude. Moreover, since every part is ordered to the whole as imperfect to perfect, and every man is part of the complete community, then law must look to the common happiness which is the common good.

Then he refers to Aristotle for support: we call those acts legally just which tend to produce and conserve happiness and its parts for the political community;[2] complete community is the city.[3] No doubt this position on the complete community (*communitas perfecta*) is an Aristotelian position and one which St. Thomas always maintains. No doubt also that it is a position which disturbs many readers. Aristotle held that the city is the comprehensive community embracing all men and all lesser communities precisely because it is their fulfillment. Only in the city does man achieve self-sufficiency, not just for living, but for living well. Living well is not merely a "more commodius life," as Hobbes would say, but a life of excellent activity, the exercise of the moral and intellectual virtues. This is the final good, and the city makes it possible.

While Artistotle accepts many "complete communities" horizontally (Athens, Sparta, Thebes), he recognizes only one vertically. Trade and defensive alliances, for instance, do not make a city. So the city takes in the whole life of man, and everything comes within its jurisdiction. Aristotle does have some limits on the functions of the city. For instance, he maintains a pluralism of communities with their proper functions (*e.g.*, in his criticism of Plato in *Politics* II) which are necessary for the city itself; and there is the contemplative activity which is somehow superhuman.[4] But the latter is not institutionalized and the former acts in subordination to the city.

Aristotle's city exists for the moral perfection of man and for its own value as the highest association. Not every city does this well, but in principle its laws should guide all areas of men's lives – education, religion, art, literature. It is a church-state. An isolated reading of I-II:90,2 might lead one to say: "Well, here we have the Aristotelian totalitarian state; in it, whole men are parts totally subordinated to the state and its laws." Anyone who knows Aquinas will say, of course, that that is not so. But how does he *systematically* avoid the conclusions of the Aristotelian premises?

First, in historical perspective, many things happened between the time of Aristotle and that of Aquinas. Before Aristotle was dead, the Alexandrian empire was well on its way with its ideal of one great Hellenic city. The empire died, but Alexander lived in idealized legend as "the Great." There was Stoicism and its "cosmopolis" in which men lived as in their natural society, governed by the immanent Reason and its "natural laws." (The Stoics seemed to tend toward social individualism with respect to the political community.) This heavily influenced Roman Law, which in the Justinian code used natural law and the law of nations as the background for civil law. There was the Roman Empire; the boast, pride, and justification of Roman imperialism was the establishment of an order of justice and peace. Most importantly, there was the Judeo-Christian revelation which, without undermining political order, proposed a way of salvation and human perfection (an ultimate end) beyond philosophy or politics. And there was Augustine who, aside from the Scriptures, was the weightiest "authority" in western Christianity. He placed classical culture and the Empire in a theology of history and salvation.

Second – and here, it seems to me, we encounter one of several instances in which Aquinas wholly accepted an Aristotelian analysis, a formal definition and structure, and yet broke out of its material identifications – in no text does he say that the part, as part, is not subordinate to the whole; that the individual man and lesser communities are not parts of the complete community; that there is more than one ultimate end for man, happiness or beatitude. There is no more social individualism in Aquinas than in Aristotle. Yet nowhere, except when quoting Aristotle, does Aquinas identify the complete community (*communitas perfecta*) with the political community. He explicitly denies that man is wholly a part of, and subordinate to, the political community.[5] And he says there are some private goods (not *qua* private, however) which are superior to the common good of the political community.[6] Where, then, is the complete community to which all those Aristotelian attributes apply?

I believe this is settled in the first article of q. 91: Is there an eternal law? Answer: Law is simply the directive of the practical reason of the ruler of some *aliqua* (indicating there may be others) *complete community*; but the whole *community of the universe* is governed by the eternal reason of God. It is this community of the universe, or more specifically, the *respublica hominum sub Deo*, which most properly and wholly deserves the title of complete community.[7] It is the primary analogate (*in se*, not *quoad nos*) from which all other communities derive their title and justification. And this is the first law to which all others are subordinate. Natural law is man's participation in eternal law through his own given teleological structure, and the capacity of his intelligence to grasp this structure and work out in more or less detail its application to human living.[8] Likewise, there is only one ultimate common good, which is God; any other common goods are ordered to that one: *Nihil firmiter constat per rationem practicam nisi per ordinationem ad ultimum finem, qui est bonum commune.*[9]

As in all cases of participation, the participants (parts) share in the communicated perfection of the whole only in a limited mode. If there are other "complete" communities, "ultimate" ends, "common" goods, they are so only in a limited order and in teleological subordination to the whole. Aquinas never specifically identifies any political community of his time as *the*, or even *a*, complete community, but some of them must be, since they have a common good and an authority to make law for the common good.[10] He seems indifferent as to whether it be a city, a province, or a kingdom.[11] He is more concerned to show the common limitations of all human law (and societies) within the total structure of law and societies.

As Aristotle and Aquinas both say, it is sometimes good method in investigating what something is, to see what it is not. The genuine values of political society and its law may best be seen by looking first at what they cannot do. So we go back to our beginning, I-II:91,4, where I think Aquinas best sums up the whole matter.

Why do men need a divine law? Isn't human reason, by its participation in the eternal law (which, after all, is a divine law), sufficient to lead men to a good life? No, for four reasons. First, man is ordained to an end which is above his natural capacity to know or achieve. The end must be revealed, and man must be directed to it by a law divinely revealed. This, of course, is the essential limitation by which Christianity has always tried to put manners on all human communities. "My kingdom is not of this world." No matter what high ideals, how fine the structures and laws, how good and beneficent the ruler, the political community is no substitute for this religion; politics is not a way of salvation. Deification of ruler, state, race, or nation is a sin against the divine good and, therefore, against *the* complete community whose common good is the divine good.

Second, on account of the incertitude of human judgment, especially in contingent and particular matters, there would be diverse judgments about good and evil in human activity and diverse and contrary laws; so that men might know without doubt what they are to do, there would be need of revelation from the unerring source of truth.[12] Aquinas maintains that all men know the common principles of natural law; they are the indemonstrable and self-evident basis for all moral science. Beyond this, there is required some work of reason in which error can enter.[13] He also holds that the decalogue is, in its content, natural moral law, and would be known by most men in its generality because it does not require much *industria rationis*.[14] As one descends to more particular issues, there is more room for error, owing to the difficulty of holding multiple facts and values together, and from wrong customs, habits, passions, etc.

This is to say that philosophy (ethics) is neither a way of salvation nor even a way for a "people" to achieve a good human life. Granted that most important ethicians are men of high moral ideals and principles in their philosophy and life, what do ordinary people (even university students) make of this great diversity of expert opinion on some of the most important moral issues they face? It easily lends itself to a subjective individualism which would result in utter chaos if it were not checked by the tendency to conformism (rooted perhaps in the need for community and a common good). It would not be a bad estimate, I think, to say that at least ninety percent of the people get the only sure moral guidance they have from religious sources, mediated by the family and by whatever there are of religious ideals in the ethos (including the laws) of their community. As a common ethos breaks down under the pressure of

pluralism and individualism, men tend to turn to political authority
and law. And, as legality becomes morality, the way is opened for a
totalitarian regime.

These first two limitations apply to natural as well as human law;
the following two seem to apply only to human law. Third, men can
judge only exterior behavior, not the interior acts which are nevertheless necessary for the perfection of virtue. Hence, law cannot
adequately check and direct interior acts, but only the exterior acts
of virtue. Aquinas always maintains that the aim (*finis*) of human
law is to make men good (*i.e.,* to lead them to a virtuous life), but
the object of human law, (*i.e.,* what it can directly command), is the
virtuous act (*agere virtuosa*). But to do the virtuous act as the virtuous man does it *(agere virtuosa virtuose)* requires choice and
habit, and human law cannot prescribe this.[15] By coercive threats,
human law can make me pay a debt, but it cannot make me an
honest man. The hope (intention) of human law is that by proposing
the ideal of good conduct and by habituating men (especially the *in-
solentes juvenes*) to such conduct through fear, they may come to
see and accept this as good way of life, *i.e.,* to become virtuous.[16]

We know very well that an external practice cannot long be sustained if it is not internalized. Whence comes this internalization?
Human political law and structures may help much to sustain it, but
they cannot bring it about. Rather, what *is* internalized, good or
bad, will eventually become the law and set the ethos of the community. The exterior is bound to be in the long run the expression
of the interior. When God says not only: You shall not kill, commit
adultery, steal; but also: You shall love your neighbor and not even
covet his wife or his goods, then a man is faced with the responsibility of righting his interior so that he may indeed be a good man.
One may of course violate both kinds of rule, but at least he knows
where he stands and has a steady reminder of his need to change.
And the believer is also offered that which alone can make him
capable of living the good life, *i.e.,* grace and the infused virtues of
faith, hope, and charity. A political society which does not foster
religious life in the community is undercutting its own best hope of
making good citizens.[17]

Fourth, and finally, human law cannot prohibit and punish all
evils; in attempting to do so it would take away many goods
necessary to the common good. This is Aquinas's protest against
excessive moralizing of human law. He has a healthy realism: men

(even under the New Law) are not all perfect in virtue; most, in fact, are quite imperfect. So if law leads them at all, it has to lead them slowly, lest if asked too much they resist and break out into greater evils.[18] Human law should proscribe only those acts of vice from which the majority are able to abstain and especially those which are injurious to others and without which human society cannot be maintained.

Human society must tolerate many evils and let much go unpunished. Of course, all acts of vice are prohibited by natural law, but the second and third limitations apply again. Only when God has spoken are men sure of what is required of them internally and externally, and of inevitable punishment for unrepented evil. That the evil seem to prosper and the good suffer is something to which men cannot reconcile themselves. But the believer knows that in the long run, in the complete community, this is not so.[19] And the certain knowledge of eventually having to pay one's debt in punishment is a powerful motivation in human life. It is not, of course, the motive of love which the New Law makes the force of Christian life, but for imperfect men it is a force without which much love and much good would be lost.[20]

All these limitations should not, of course, lead one to think that Aquinas belittles political community. In fact, he considers it the greatest work of human practical reason,[21] a positive good ordained by God and a necessary, if not sufficient, condition for a good human life.[22] So a brief word is in order about its positive functions and the Christian attitude toward it.

Aquinas says that human law may command those acts of any virtue which can be referred to the common good either immediately (e.g. defense of the city) or mediately.[23] The latter category refers to measures taken to form the citizens in good habits by which they are disposed to maintain the common good of justice and peace. This opens a wide area and one would have to work through many texts to see what Aquinas might approve in the way of civil law, a task beyond the scope of this essay. However, one thing may be said: since according to Aquinas it is a special function of political authority to care for distributive justice,[24] it would seem legitimate for it to regulate property, wealth, and social structure to assure all citizens of the opportunity to share equitably in the goods of the community.

In view of the limitations he places on political society and law,

one must conclude that Aquinas would tend to a minimalist interpretation of state intervention. The state should act firmly but infrequently. Its job seems rather to promote the orderly functioning
of the other communities which produce the common goods, and to
intervene only in such matters as cannot or in fact are not being
cared for by other communities. This requires the highest kind of
prudence. In spite of the Aristotelian definitions, Aquinas seems,
with regard to political community, to follow more the Roman func-
tional conception, *i.e.* that the state is to maintain
an order of justice and peace within which men in their other associations can carry on their work and growth in reasonable
security.

Aquinas systematically sustains a long Christian tradition that
political authority and law bind in conscience.[25] The divine order
manifested in the social nature of man calls him to political community, to develop those social and legal structures necessary to
secure the opportunity to develop the natural human potentialities.
The New Law does not destroy but gives a new dimension and perfection to the natural structure. Without undue "moralizing" in the
sense we have already considered, Aquinas places human law and
political order firmly within the total moral order. Politics and law
are not games to be played, as some legal positivists would have it;
they engage the moral conscience and personality of the citizen.
Not even the Holy Spirit can exempt one from political
community.[26]

Yet the conditions for human law being binding in conscience
take us back to the limitations of law. To have moral force the law
must be equitable, within the jurisdiction of the enacting authority,
and a needed means to the common good. A law directly contrary
to natural or divine law is by that very fact beyond the jurisdiction
of political authority, and so not binding. Such "laws" are not laws;
they are acts of violence.[27]

So, for the Christian, politics is neither all-important nor unimportant. He will engage in it conscientiously according to need, opportunity, and ability. But he will not expect from it perfect justice
and peace, nor perfect happiness and salvation. And he will be
watchful that it not pervert the very order which justifies it by
usurping jurisdiction where there is a higher law in force. This is a
difficult task at any time. Perhaps today, with our pluralism of
competing values, it requires even greater competence and firmer

moral virtue. But the Christian has the resources, and he cannot let politics fall to the perverters by default.

Notes

¹ Cf. St. Thomas Aquinas, *Summa Theologica* I. 1. 3-8 and *loca parallela*.

² Aristotle, *Ethics* V. 1.

³ Artistotle, *Politics* I. 1.

⁴ *Ethics* X. 7-8.

⁵ Aquinas, *Summa* I-II. 21.4, ad 3; cf. Aquinas, *In X Eth.*, XI, #2101 (an interpretation of Artistotle on the life of contemplation).

⁶ *Summa* I-II. 113. 9 · ad 2; II-II. 152.4, ad 3; nor is man totally subordinated to the good of the universe: cf. I-II. 2. 8, ad 2.

⁷ *Summa* I-II. 100.5 *(communitas seu respublica hominum sub Deo)*; 21.4 *(tota communitas universi)*; II-II. 40.4 *(respublica fidelium)*. On God as the common good of man and the universe, cf. I-II. 109.3; II-II. 26.3; *Summa Contra Gentiles* III. 17; *De Perfectione Vitae Spiritualis* 13.634.

⁸ *Summa* I-II. 91.2; 92.2 and 4.

⁹ *Ibid.*, I-II. 90.2, ad 3.

¹⁰ This is implied in the whole area of human law, I-II. 95-97, but especially in 95.4 and 96.1.

¹¹ *Summa* II-II. 40.1 This article on war seems to call for further specification. The first condition for a just war is that it be waged by the authority of the ruler (princeps); a private person cannot wage war because he can appeal to a superior to prosecute his rights. So war is a matter for the ruler of the city, kingdom, or province. Do dukes, princes, and even kings have no superior? What about the Holy Roman Emperor or the Papa Imperator?

¹² Aquinas returns frequently to the many reasons why God reveals matters which in principle are knowable by the resources of human reason; cf. I. 1. 1; *C.G.* I.4; I-II. 99.2, ad 2; II-II. 22.1, ad 1 and 22.4.

¹³ *Summa* I-II. 94.2 and 4.

¹⁴ *Ibid.*, 100.1 and 3.

¹⁵ *Ibid.*, 92.1; 95.1; 96.3, ad 2; 100.2.

¹⁶ Cf. *Ibid.*, I-II. 95.1; 96.3, ad 2.

¹⁷ Aquinas remarks that although human law is not concerned with divine cult in itself, yet even the gentiles make some laws about sacred matters as it seemed helpful to the moral formation of the citizens for the common good (I-II. 99.3). Nevertheless, unbelievers are not to be compelled to pro-

fess the faith (II-II. 10.8).

[18] *Ibid.*, I-II. 96.2, ad 2.

[19] *Ibid.*, I-II. 21.4; II. 64.2, ad 1.

[20] Yves Simon has explained well the function of coercion and fear in the formation of good habits; see *Philosophy of Democratic Government* (Chicago: University of Chicago Press, 1951), pp. 108-112.

[21] Aquinas, *In Lib. Pol.*, Proem, #7.

[22] *Summa* I-II. 95.1 and 2; 96.4.

[23] *Ibid.*, I-II. 96.3.

[24] *Ibid.*, I. 1.21. c and ad 3; II-II. 61.1, ad 3.

[25] *Ibid.*, I-II. 96.4.

[26] *Ibid.*, 96.5. This is a highly nuanced statement.

[27] *Ibid.*, 96.4. c and ad 2; 93.3, ad 2; 95.2.

The Medieval Beginnings of
Political Secularization

Thomas Molnar

IN THIS ESSAY I shall reflect upon the remarkable process by which
political theory detached itself from Christian political presuppositions – not in modern times, as it is genererally believed, but
already in the late Middle Ages, long before Machiavelli. I was indeed tempted to discuss such pairs as Machiavelli and Hobbes,
Spinoza and Rousseau, Maistre and Mill, Hegel and Marx – all of
whom are regarded as par excellence theoreticians of modernism
in political thought. Nevertheless, I decided to present to you some
medieval elements of the later open conflict between Christian and
modernist thinking. My chief reason is that the issues, while they
may seem more remote from the twentieth-century student,
display the clash in what we would regard today as non-ideological
terms, thus showing us that we deal in modern times with concepts
deeply imbedded in western political thought. The overall issue
was – and is – whether the State can exist as a well-ordered entity
without the spiritual power playing in it an *institutional* function.

The Christian Middle Ages received a brilliant but also difficult
heritage. Simplifying matters, we can say that the political issue in
ancient times centered around the State, which existed as an un-
problematic entity, propitiating the municipal pantheon and sure of
its citizens' devotion (or, at least, obedience) since they too depended on the good will of the same gods.[1] Christianity turned upside
down this stable arrangement. First of all, there were now two
spheres, the spiritual and the temporal, and thus two supreme ruling and governing entities, Church and State. They were both

divinely willed and created. In the second place, their relationship
was full of conflicts of a historical, theological, and finally political
nature. And third: the very fact of these conflicts created circumstances in which new entities could also emerge, allied now to
the State against the Church, then to Church against State, until
such time when these new entities – feudal lords, early communes,
burghers, humanists, clerics – became self-reliant and entered the
fray on their own.

Let us turn now with more attention to the second point, the relationship between State (king, emperor) and Church (papacy,
bishops, religious orders, outstanding abbots).

With the fall of the Western Roman Empire, the papacy too suffered a certain eclipse. In fact, for centuries afterward it was surrounded by hostile forces taking advantage of the Church's political
weakness, as well as of the fact that under the protection of the
Eastern emperors some powerful patriarchs in Constantinople all
but challenged the authority of the Bishop of Rome. An unexpected
but well-seized opportunity presented itself for Rome when Pepin
and Charlemagne became powerful rulers of the Franks.
Charlemagne decisively defeated the Lombards who had threatened central Italy, and had himself crowned by the Pope at
Christmas, 800. Two consequences are noteworthy: the idea of the
"Roman Empire" again materialized in the West, under
Charlemagne and his successors, then under a long line of
emperors of the Holy Roman-Germanic Empire; and the Church,
under periodically emerging strong pontiffs – Gregory VII, Innocent III, Boniface VIII – was able to become the equal, even the
superior, partner of the emperors in governing and inspiring the
Christian world, the *respublica christiana.*

Politics penetrates every part of human relationships, as it did
the one between the two heads of the medieval Christian world.
The problem which now presented itself – and did not go away until
the eclipse of the papacy as a worldly power, in the sixteenth century – was the following: at the beginning, in the centuries between
the eighth and eleventh, the secular power prevailed, due partly to
the emperor's prestige and partly to the emerging feudal system.
Both of these were now feared and respected by a populace saved
from the turbulent times of barbarian invasions. Thanks to the set-
tling of people inside the new order, and to papal authority, a
renaissance of ecclesiastical power occurred, clearly noticeable in

the gothic art forms where God's greatness is celebrated in stone and stained glass. Contrary to the style of celebration (in art, for example, in the mosaics of Ravenna) prevailing in the Eastern Empire, where the emperor is depicted as a semi-divine figure, emperors and kings in the West are represented as receiving their power from God, and as standing hierarchically under the celestial ranks. A late echo of this state of things may be perceived in the writings of Bishop Bossuet, at the zenith-time of royal absolutism, in the seventeenth century: "The power of kings comes from above, yet they must not think that they are masters of this power, using it at their whim; they are compelled to use it with fear and moderation, since God will demand an account." And even more forcefully: "Kings must tremble while using their God-given powers, and think how horrible is the sacrilege of using such a power for evil."[2]

Two factors were at work, from about the thirteenth century on, to weaken the ecclesiastical hold. Ultimately, they were to result in what Georges de Lagarde, author of a vast synthesis of late medieval thought, calls the "birth of the lay spirit."[3] The first drive originated within the religious order itself, the so-called mendicant orders. Although conceived as Christian militias and servants of the Church – they indeed fulfilled this role – they became quasi-independent centers of speculation, conduct, and artistic representation, and, of importance to us here, focuses of thought on the relationship with the secular world. This is how art and social historian Georges Duby describes this evolution: "Through sermons, through theatrical representations, through various means of direct action, the mendicant orders began to detach the faithful from the Church, conceived as a rival. They reinvigorated the anti-clerical tendencies of the heretical movements, the same ones they had had the mission to combat and rally to the orthodoxy, and whose resurgence they now blocked."[4] Among these mendicant orders, especially the Franciscans (or rather a branch, the so-called Fraticelli), some began to challenge (unsuccessfully) essential doctrines of the Church. But other Franciscans, such as William of Ockham, succeeded in formulating and accrediting the notion that the secular ruler need not submit to the spiritual power – in other words, that secular power has no religious basis.[5]

With this statement, we have named the second factor which was to weaken the Church's position of supremacy in the Christian West. The medieval question (Whence the state's power?) received various answers. For instance, the feudal lords replied: From the power of the sword, from wars; the doctors of the Church: It is God who delegates their power to kings; the pope: Power comes from God, but through the mediation of St. Peter and his successor. If we discount the first answer as not within the scope of Christian speculation, we still find a deep controversy between the latter two propositions – and, as we shall see, an additional one – which invoke God as the source of royal (or imperial) power. God delegates his powers, but does he do so via the Church (pope) or directly? After all, there was the Roman Empire, a pagan one, into which Christ and the Apostles were born, and which they accepted (one of them, Paul, being a citizen of it). Long before Peter was born, there were emperors and empires; thus temporal rule can be said to antedate the Church, equal with it in power and independence, both depending, although through separate channels, directly on God's creation and sustaining will.[6]

This debate was not only a theological one; it also cut into the flesh of high political interests as well as of daily affairs. Its various interpretations meant a positive or a negative answer to such questions as whether, for reasons of *political* disobedience, the pope had the right to excommunicate the emperor; whether the bishops had the right to independent secular possessions and dominations, even privileges; whether members of the clergy may have recourse to ecclesiastical courts; and so on. The secular side in these and other matters came to be represented by the new class of lawyers who studied Roman law at the new university of Bologna, and by such theological-legalists as William of Ockham and Marsilius of Padua. In combination – that is, of the theological and historical/legal arguments – they were validating the emperor's cause, and ultimately the cause of secularization.

From the enormous literature generated by this network of conflict and controversy, we can attempt to disengage only a few major themes. The most important of these was the trend to oppose the Church's power and ubiquitous influence by referring to the original, "evangelical" poverty (upheld by radical Franciscans and the heretical sects), and by the effort to rehabilitate the Roman concept of law and State as an alternative to the prevailing mode of thought. The first issue never received a "solution," although it was to be taken up by the Reformers who criticized the Church's wealth, pomp and ceremony. It was the second issue which grew into an enormous tidal wave, since all sorts of interests and aspirations found themselves represented in it. There is no question that the lawyers carried the major part of the attack against the Church's secular power and ecclesiastical property: they represented the aggressive secularization drive of Frederick II, the Hohenstaufen emperor; of the French kings, relieved of the imperial pressure at the death of Frederick; of the Italian communes which wanted to impose town-taxes and their own jurisdiction on the clerics; and so on. These issues received theoretical support from political thinkers and from the early humanists. The first argued, with Aristotle, that the State is a natural thing; that the emperor receives the power of the sword from God (Simon of Bisignano, end of the twelfth century); that the king, even if crowned by a priest, still governs a human institution (Ockham, early fourteenth century); etc. The second, the humanists, did not put forth arguments, but studied rather the ancient political and legal literature of Rome, and concluded that that society (the pagan-Roman) was purely secular, yet well-ordered and efficiently governed. They went even farther when they discovered in the second-century Roman jurist, Ulpian, that public law in Rome referred also to sacred things and that priests were appointed to what amounts to civil service ("civil" and "sacred" being naturally confused in Roman public philosophy). Thus reference to Roman law had the effect of releasing "the Christian ruler from ecclesiological encumbrances by secularizing his government's foundations."[7]

According to W. Ullmann's somewhat exaggerated thesis, the consultation of ancient literature was prompted by the twin ambitions to desacralize religious man – to restore, as Ullmann puts it, the original, pre-Christian, unregenerated man – and to restore also the concept of politics as an independent category of thought and area of action. He states his conviction that the *studia humanitatis*, that is, humanism before and during the Renaissance, was no more than an auxiliary science in this endeavor, really an outgrowth of the attempts to secure for the ruler his emancipation from ecclesiastical tutelage.[8] While this is an exaggeration, the fact is that a man who was both a humanist and a student of law, Marsilius of Padua, effected the final junction between the various opponents of the Church's power. His treatise, *Defensor Pacis*, has a deceptively simple thesis: the "peace" that must be defended is that of the entire Christian community threatened by the Church's claim to spiritual authority. But Christ gave the Church no "power of the keys," he himself was no "king of kings," and therefore the pope should have no secular power either. He is a mere usurper, even in his claim to rule over the clergy. Instead, priests and popes ought to be subject to election by the people; they should be subject to secular power. For, after all, the Christian community as a whole is the only reliable legislator, judge, and interpreter of doctrine. The "spiritual power" is a dangerous device to split the community; all power is vested in the people and its elected rulers.

One can see even from this brief summary that Marsilius stood at the dead center of diffuse radical doctrines which preceded his time and the more easily identifiable political theories afterwards, those of Machiavelli, Hobbes, Rousseau with their "civil religion," up to our own radical critics of the spiritual authority. Such theses were put forward, as has been said before, by the emperor's and king's lawyers, in part to safeguard the secular ruler's theoretical power base. In this endeavor, the lawyers were justified. But with Marsilius and afterwards, the legitimate self-defense of the secular ruler against ecclesiastical encroachment degenerated into an *ideology*, a radical affirmation of one cause, and an enterprise of demolition of the rival cause. The issue which had arisen with the birth of Christianity – whether man is a citizen of two realms rather than of only the tangible, secular one – received from these thinkers an indignantly negative answer: the political community excludes all others; what is called "spiritual" must be equally determined and articulated by the secular power. This is, in essence, the basis of "modernist" political thought, a "civil religion," the ideology of the community, organized by and for the community, a denial of transcendence. Hence the infatuation with the pagan State in general: with the ancient pagan State on the part of the medieval lawyers, with the contemporary idea of the pagan State on the part of modern ideologues. And hence the exaltation of the ruler (by Marsilius, Machiavelli, Hobbes, etc.) and his endowment with absolute power.

Marsilius is popularly credited with the conciliar thesis, namely, that real power in the Church should not belong to the pope, not even to any segment of the clergy, but to the representatives of all Christendom, assembled in council. Nor should the pope have the monopoly of calling together such an assembly; only the emperor should have that power, and the results of the deliberations should have a binding effect on the pope. It is obvious, however, that the objective of Marsilius is not the establishment of a mere ecclesiastical democracy but, far beyond that, the creation of a kind of totalitarian rule in which people's spiritual aspirations may flow through only one channel: the one determined by the ruler, or, in the modern sense of the word, by the State. As de Lagarde writes: "Up to Marsilius, nobody thought of denying the reality of a spiritual power and to contest its competence in the properly religious domain. It was Marsilius's own contribution to negate the very existence and possibility of a spiritual power."[9]

In spite of the radicalism of Marsilius and of his ideological mind-structure, we must be very careful in discerning the various motives for his attacks against the Church, as well as for similar attacks by others. There was the ubiquity of Church penetration into secular life which irritated the powerful and analytical minds nurtured carefully by the institutions of the Church. There was the often strained relationship, reminiscent of feudal relationships, between the Church and the various religious orders, which were extremely powerful, quasi-independent centers of power. This developed at times into a competition, not only between Church and religious order, but also among the orders themselves, each claiming for its missions and functions a specially exalted status. Among the contenders were the secular rulers, the towns, by now rich and strong, independent sources of influence, taking sides in the ecclesiastical rivalries and even influencing them. And there was, last but not least, the desire of Italian patriots (among them, members of the clergy) to weaken the pope's secular power in the peninsula, to incite the emperor to fight the pope, and thus to achieve the liberation and unification of Italy as a state no longer dominated by the Church. Both William of Ockham and Marsilius sought refuge at one point at the court of Emperor Louis of Bavaria, and when Ockham took up his pen in the defense of the latter's cause, it was both as a representative of anti-papal Franciscans *and* as a philosophical exponent of the ruler's secular base.

Such men as Ockham and Marsilius achieved an easy popularity in the eyes of posterity. It may seem, indeed, that their ambition was eminently humane and reasonable, even genuinely spiritual, for the good of the Church and of the State. The impression we form of their life-work is that they aimed, first of all, at *separating* what was previously, if not united, at least intertwined by historical contingencies, such as the temporal and the spiritual spheres, and at *safeguarding* the function and independence of both. They are supposed to have proposed ways of purifying religion, cutting away the weeds, such as power-hunger, accumulation of wealth, interference and conflict with secular interests. Thus Professor A.S. McGrade argues that William of Ockham merely advocated "a less juridical and more spiritual ecclesiastical government,"[10] and Professor Alan Gewirth suggests that Marsilius gave only an early outline of a democratic regime.[11]

The truth is much more complex, and perhaps less favorable to the family of thinkers represented by the above two. Ockham's philosophy was a subjectivist one, the kind that medieval scholastic terminology called "nominalistic." Even Professor McGrade, otherwise a partisan of Ockham, admits that this subjectivity had the effect of depriving politics of a theological, and we might add, of a rational, foundation. What does this mean? Nominalism rejects the real existence of so-called universals; it proposes, in other words, that there is no such thing as mankind, only individual men and women; no such thing as friendship, only friendly attitudes between two or more persons. If that is so, then State, Church, corporations, institutions, etc. are not *real* either; politics is reduced to empirically observable acts that the weakness of our minds tends to group under names which remain empty of content (*flatus vocis*). Thus the proper actors of the political sphere are concrete individuals with here-and-now interests, not corporate wholes. It follows that the area of politics is exclusively that of the secular power – whose motions and motives can be empirically ascertained – and that the spiritual authority has no place in it. The king's power is conferred by men who see to it that the minimal goals of secular government are attained, and they are generally successful in so doing because king and subjects are reasonable people.

Ockham was, of course, a religious man. He recognized the specificity of spiritual power which, although it had no empirical basis, was appointed by God. It is on God's will, on revelation and on the Bible, that spiritual authority rests, and this was enough to validate it in Ockham's eyes. But suppose there comes along a man less pious than the great Franciscan thinker, a Marsilius, for example. He will pay no more than lip service to the Bible, thus removing any and all justification of spiritual power. The latter remains dangling, and not only is it then subordinated to the empirically verifiable secular sphere; its specificity is also denied and confiscated for the secular sphere in the form of a secular/spiritual religion, or as we would say today, an ideology.

This was the consequence of the many-pronged movement to emancipate the State from Church interference. The question now is, did not the attack on spiritual power, in itself and for its role in the secular area, erode also the status of the temporal power, the State? At first sight, it seems that the State as such was the winner of the conflict. As John of Paris saw it, rulership was no longer the effluence of grace, and therefore there was no need for the priest's mediating role: everything that the political realm needed was already there. Government belonged to the natural community, the State. As creator of nature, God had endowed nature with its own laws, one of which concerned the establishment of the State and its government. Nothing was left that could be mediated. As far as the Church was concerned, the same John of Paris logically held that it was a *purely mystical* body, having nothing to do with the *purely natural* body politic. The function of its ministers is not half-political, it is exclusively sacramental.

We should argue, naturally, that the *separation* effected by such medieval thinkers as Simon of Bisignano, William of Ockham, John of Paris, Marsilius of Padua, and others weakened the status of the spiritual authority, but it also undermined the power of the State that the separation was to make independent of the spiritual authority. No community can stand without the spiritual element (which is also the civilizing element) integrated with its existence and structure. The secular State as such, whether it is the medieval one or the modern liberal or Marxist one, is able to generate out of its entrails a merely ersatz spirituality (ideology) which works not at its preservation, but at its destruction. However, the other issue at this point of our historical-political analysis is that the concept of the State itself suffered at the hands of those whose aim had been to strengthen it.

What kind of concept of the State was elaborated by the emperor's and king's partisans? The citizens were assumed to be men of reason and justice, and, as Marsilius had it, their assemblies were supposed to constitute the surest body of legislators – to such an extent that they were also to legislate the correct interpretation of doctrine, this time as assemblies of believers. Following Marsilius, Wyclif, who was also an opponent of the visible Church, suggested that churchmen should enter the ruler's sphere of obedience and that only the ruler possesses the right to exclude (that is, to excommunicate) any member from what would be then a spiritualized (ideological) community. The question is: can the State, saddled with spiritual or quasi-spiritual or pseudo-spiritual responsibilities, still remain a State? Did the predecessors and followers of Marsilius not grant the State a poisoned gift when they radicalized its function beyond all measure? Perhaps they thought they were putting an end to a grievous mixture of rules and responsibilities with the far-reaching separation of Church and State. But the flaw in their thinking was evident when they conceived the Church as a purely mystical body: the state thus governed the secular domain but faced powers too heavy for it to shoulder.

The second flaw was of a purely political character. On the surface and in good faith, the beneficiary of the changes should have been the secular ruler. The monarchic principle was taken for granted by medieval thinkers who were leaning on both the biblical and the classical precepts in this area, and also on the Roman precedent. Even Bishop Bossuet was to write in the seventeenth century that Rome ought not to have abolished its kingdom and turned into a republic because, after several hundred years, it proved that much harder to return to the monarchy, that of the Caesars. Yet, was it the ruler (the State) whose position was now strengthened at the end of the conflict between spiritual and temporal? In practice and for a while, yes; but the theoretical undermining proceeded apace. Not only was the ruler to be elected by the people; the laws, too, were the expression of the people's will. And since the people follow their natural desires, they cannot enact laws which are unjust! Nature itself restricts the bad exercise of popular sovereignty! (Marsilius). The same naturalism (and optimism) is found in Ockham: "natural equity" suffices to regulate human affairs if (*sic*) men lived reasonably.

Imperceptibly, then, the "defense of peace" (from the meddling of the spiritual authority) became a contradictory position: the secular State was itself divided between ruler and people – an ambiguous division, since the first no longer had a spiritual authority behind him, while the second did not have the instruments (for example, democratic representation) to make its will known. With all its imperfections, the earlier system was at least coherent: the people were united by the Christian faith represented and guided by a visible Church; and they were governed by a ruler who shared their faith. In the proposed dispensation the *consent* was left either to the ruler's ability to enforce Christianity or any other system of belief (anticipating Machiavelli's central thesis) – an enforced consent – or to the "reasonableness" of the citizens agreeing, in their "natural equity," to legislate for the public good.

The two flaws I just distinguished in the position of Ockham, Marsilius, John of Paris, and other radical thinkers of the Middle Ages have resulted in two permanent themes running through the political course of subsequent centuries, up to the present. Let me again formulate the first flaw: the conception of the Church as a purely mystical body, which justifies its exclusion from the life of the *civitas*, the political life. Most religious systems which have deviated from the Church during these centuries assumed, indeed, that by her true vocation the Church ought to be aloof from politics, the alternative being an immoral, power-hungry ecclesiastical construct, a political pressure group. *Tertium non datur*, as witness the line running from the Lutheran controversy in the sixteenth century to the progressive theologians of Vatican II, who refer, in a condemnatory manner, to the Church as "Constantinian."

Thus, the emphasis, from the fourteenth to the twentieth centuries, has been on the separation of Church from State: the Church was to be limited to the private sphere of charismatic groups, or as they are called in France, *groupes de recherche*, forever redefining what Christianity is about; the State was expected to lead the citizens to secular virtues. The overall consequence of these two positions was to fill the political space, from which the Church had been excluded, with the State's ideology; the State became a substitute Church, and in certain instances, logically, a totalitarian regime.

Let me now define the second flaw: the supremacy of the people who should elect the ruler (and the pope), and also choose the laws by which they want to be governed. A shorter formula for this is popular sovereignty, and the only suitable institutional framework, democracy. As with the first theme, the Church as a mystical body, here too the consequence is the secularization of society, since the choice of laws and the selection of the ruler gradually become processes of diminishing moral return, as witnessed by us during the recent decades. This time not the State, but society is entrusted with the formulation of the ideology which is to preside both at lawmaking and at the election of officials.

Thus the conclusion reached by the radical medieval thinkers and their modern disciples is the elimination of the Church as the spiritually and morally ordering principle in State and society. They expected, instead, that State or society will produce the ordering principle, a purely secular morality, exemplified in the doctrines of free masonry and ethical culture society. From Machiavelli to Rousseau, from Hobbes to Hegel, the modernist political philosophers constructed the model of the ideological State.

The error of these conceptions is the denial of the Church's corporate nature, a principle that the Church follows in various associations that it organizes. The authors of these conceptions have been intent on rehabilitating the pagan State, modelled after an ideal Athens and an ideal Rome, where the *numenon* (which is by no means the same as the transcendental) was built into the State's temporal structure. Hence, independent religious endeavors had to lead an underground existence, or they were incorporated with official worship. The first course was chosen in Athens by the orphic cults, the second by the orphic-pythagorean beliefs assimilated by decree of the Roman senate in the fourth century B.C. to the official cult of the State.

The phenomenon of Christianity changed the scope and relationship of the temporal and the spiritual, that is, of State and Church. Just as grace does not abolish nature but brings it to its highest expression, so the supernatural that entered the life of men through Christianity did not abolish the State (or man's political nature); it mobilized the State for the function of promoting Christian life. As Thomas Aquinas put it, the State is a *communitas perfectissima* for the realization of man's faculties, although it is not a final end.

Yet, clearly, the State is not a Church; its task is not to lead men to salvation, but only to facilitate virtuous life through the orderliness that it seeks and imposes on human transactions through laws and well-ordered values. Good laws and obedience to them *are not* the same as Christian life. They promote it in sufficient measure for man thereafter to reach salvation, which is the function of the spiritual/moral institution, the Church. The latter cannot be excluded from public life because then the State reverts back to the pagan ideal and the pagan structure. Nor can the citizenry be entrusted with formulating laws without the right moral guidance, since man's fallen nature tempts him to legalize the unvirtuous.

For all these reasons, the medieval radical concepts embodied in the *Defensor Pacis* and other works have led, in their subsequent and increasingly secularized versions, to the present neo-pagan State. Hence, better perhaps than the medieval critics of these concepts, we are today in the position to understand the need for the active presence and participation of the Church in the affairs of State and society.

Notes

[1] As Fustel de Coulanges argued in the *Ancient City* (La Cité Antique), ancient religion centered around the hearth and its gods. The "state religion" was an extended version of this piety.

[2] Bishop Bossuet, *Politique tirée des propres paroles del'Ecriture sainte*, III. 3. 4, p. 70. See also Jean Baechler, *Le pouvoir pur* (Paris: Calmann-Levy, 1978), where the author argues that governing under the "grace of God," the kings implicitly recognized a higher authority under which they stood.

[3] Georges de Lagarde, *La naissance de l'esprit laique*, 5 vols. (Louvain/Paris: Ed. Nauwelaerts, 1956).

[4] Georges Duby, *Le temps des cathedrales* (Paris: Gallimard, 1976), p. 266. It must be added that it was under the pontificate and powerful inspiration of Pope Gregory VII that the Church launched a great offensive against the worldly type religion developed in the previous centuries. Gregory preached humility and Christian virtues, setting off evangelical movements of all sorts, out of which arose the mendicant orders, as well as the heretical sects.

[5] More correctly, religious basis, yes, insofar as it is derived from God, but not dependent on the papacy.

[6] Some writers went so far as to suggest that the pope submit to the emperor the way Christ submitted to Pilate's judgment.

[7] Walter Ullmann, *Medieval Foundations of Renaissance Humanism*

(Ithaca: Cornell University Press, 1977), p. 51.

[8] Ullmann, *op. cit.*, p. 169.

[9] de Lagarde, *La naissance de l'esprit laique*, 3:303, 381.

[10] A. S. McGrade, *The Political Thought of William of Ockham* (Cambridge: Cambridge University Press, 1974), p. 149.

[11] Alan Gewirth, *Marsilius of Padua, The Defender of Peace* (New York: Columbia University Press, 1956).

Classical and Christian Dimensions
of American Political Thought

Ellis Sandoz

I SHALL HERE TAKE the advice of William James and try to apply it
to the American political experience. He wrote:

> Place yourself . . . at the center of a man's philosophic vision and you
> understand at once all the different things it makes him write or say.
> But keep outside, use your post-mortem method, try to build the
> philosophy up out of the single phrases, taking first one and then
> another and seeking to make them fit, and of course you fail. You
> crawl over the thing like a myopic ant over a building, tumbling into
> every microscopic crack or fissure, finding nothing but inconsisten-
> cies, and never suspecting that a center exists.[1]

What is this vision, where this center, if one seeks them in James-
ian fashion? It is the synthesis authoritatively expressed by the
generation of Founding Fathers, preeminently but not exclusively
in the familiar words of the Declaration and Constitution. The key
elements accord with the crucial insights of classical and Christian
thought and give them renewed force in the emergent nation. Jefferson and John Adams called the amalgam "the dictates of reason
and pure Americanism."[2] The self-interpretive symbols of
American nationhood denoted in the quoted phrase look in two
directions: toward the truth of man's existence personally, socially,
and historically, on the one hand, and toward the persuasive and
evocative articulation of that truth in the foundation myth of the
new community, on the other hand. In short, the articulation by
reason of the truth of Americanism is a rearticulation of the ex-

istential and transcendental truth of the Western civilization, of which America is representative. The vision at the center of American politics, then, is structured by insights into human reality taken to be universally valid for all mankind, even as they are adapted to the concrete conditions of time and place at the moment of the articulation of the new nation as an entity politically organized for action in history.[3]

Neither the pragmatic nor the purely parochial aspects of the Founding should be permitted to obscure the universalist elements: in human experience, the universal is encountered only in concrete and particular events which existentially form the participatory reality of men's lives in the In-Between of time and eternity, birth and death. This tensional reality of existence in the In-Between (including the apperceptive insights that the Whole is structured by the indices of immanence and transcendence, and that the development of human existence in time is a directional process unfolding historically and ontologically from a divine Beginning toward an equally divine goal of fulfillment) composed the consciousness of the human beings who essayed the Founding as heirs of classical philosophers and of Christian civilization. To be sure, the Founders were heirs to other influences of cardinal importance as well, such as the Old Whig or Country "ideology" of English politics so meticulously explored by Bernard Bailyn and other scholars. But the larger framework of the American vision reached beyond Plymouth and Jamestown, beyond the institutional and theoretical structures of Anglo-American civilization, and even of Western civilization itself as conventionally understood. And it was the contemporary recognition of this universal reach of their vision which explains the Founders' sense of exclusiveness and election, rather than ethnocentricity, tribalism, or simple nationalism. John Pocock has from time to time argued that, so far from being the first act of modernity, "the American Revolution and Constitution . . . form the last act of the civic Renaissance. . . ."[4] He might better have said that they form the rebirth of classical and medieval constitutionalism. For though influenced and conditioned by all that had gone before it, the thought of the Founders sought its headwaters in the oldest traditions of the civilization and partook in no essential way of the currents of radical secularist modernity already swirling around them.

The warp and woof of American political thought in the period from 1761-1791 was the movement toward truth and virtue and the quest for a just and stable order in the wake of the Revolution.[5] The standards of these several goals, and others they subsume such as liberty, equality, and happiness, were supplied by the great tradition of Western thought now revalidated. The sense in which this assessment is true can be established through an illustrative analysis of our subject matter.

Revolutionary Perspective

FOR THE PURPOSES of this discussion, the American Revolution may be considered to be a meaningful complex of experiences and symbolisms articulated with especial force and clarity during the thirty-year period just indicated. The spectrum of understanding here summarized ranges from self-interpretation by the actors and contemporaries to the level of theoretical formulation. Since, however, the American Revolution was enacted and reflected upon by persons often deeply rooted in the controlling theoretical symbolisms of philosophy and revelation, the self-interpretive end of the spectrum necessarily partakes of theoretical formulation, and the lines of distinction blur.

From the founding of the nation through the Declaration of Independence (explicit in the opening line: "When . . . one people [N.B.!] . . . dissolve[s] the political bands which have connected them with another. . . .") to the framing of the Constitution and its exegesis by Publius in the *Federalist,* to the declaration of "the great rights of mankind secured under this Constitution" in the Bill of Rights, the Revolution is dominated by actions intended to restore a true and just social and political order.[6] The *restorative* dimension of the Revolutionary experience is, therefore, dominant and determinative. It is adumbrated in the deeds and language of lawyers, politicians, and preachers, *i.e.*, by the intellectual leadership of the country. The rights, privileges and immunities of the free men of the English colonies were being systematically violated and had to be restored. The English constitution was perverted by multiple means, to the end that balance among the Estates had been destroyed and liberty itself thereby imperilled. Political influence and corruption were but palpable manifestations of the deeper spiritual malaise of *sin* and iniquity whose rot portended divine retribution unless the people (individually and collectively) repented, prayed for forgiveness, and returned to Christ in humility and faith. "The Biblical conception of a people standing in direct daily relation to God, upon covenanted terms and therefore responsible for their moral conduct," Perry Miller wrote, "was a common possession of the Protestant peoples" who overwhelmingly comprised the country's population.[7] The general sentiment of the times was that America was a land blessed of Divine Providence, inhabited by a Chosen People, led through Divine Grace by Christian men of heroic stature. And, while repentance for iniquity, constant struggle with temptation and evil of every form, and fasting and prayerful supplication for forgiveness and fortitude must accompany her every step, America's righteousness and adherence to the true faith must inevitably bring the reward of victory over Great Britain and a high place in history such as can only be achieved by the godly among nations.

The union of the temporal and spiritual communities on these general terms might be illustrated in countless ways. The intimate connection is perhaps best suggested by the practice of the Continental Congress's repeatedly calling upon the fledgling nation to observe days of "publick humiliation, fasting and prayer" as well as days of "thanksgiving." One such occasion was decided upon even prior to declaring independence, on June 12, 1775, when a communication was sent from Philadelphia to the thirteen colonies and published in newspapers and handbills that called for observance of a day of public humiliation on July 20:

> . . . that we may with united hearts and voices unfeignedly confess and deplore our many sins, and offer up our joint supplications to the all-wise, omnipotent, and merciful Disposer of all events; humbly beseeching him to forgive our iniquities, to remove our present calamities, to avert those desolating judgments with which we are threatened. . . .[8]

The ritualistic form of this resolution, adopted unanimously by Congress, involves a national confession of sin, followed by repentance, supplication for forgiveness, and prayer that punishment be stayed. Clearly expressed is the pathos of the emergent people which experienced itself as – beyond the personal hope of salvation of individuals who have entered into covenant with their maker – "explicitly merged with the society's covenant" with the " 'great Governor' " of Creation in a "living sense of a specific bond between the nation and God."[9]

Thus the dynamic of the fall from faith and restoration to grace visibly traced in revolutionary events defined the substance of man's existence in the world for Americans of this age. The immediate experiential power arose from its universality among people of a Christian nation who eagerly and fervently hoped for redemption and peace despite lapses and frailty. Corruption of religion and its restoration through the Reformation is a major motif of modern European history. The restoration sought was conceived to be to the purity of the original foundation of the church by Jesus and the Apostles. Similarly, the Renaissance was a restoration or rebirth of learning to the level attained also in distant antiquity. The cycle of fall and restoration was repeatedly enacted in English politics in the seventeenth and eighteenth centuries, from Coke onwards, with appeals even beyond *Magna Carta* (itself a restoration) to the ancient constitution, whose misty immemorial beginnings lay in the Saxon forests of the fifth century (Jefferson) or, perchance, in the remnant of settlers led by the mythical Brutus of Troy to ancient Albion's shore (Coke). The eternal and natural law, safeguarded in timeless custom, assured justice and the liberty due freemen. Politics as such was an embedded dimension of the natural order of reality whose hierarchical texture was epitomized in man's existential participation in history and being, as Aristotle's analysis of composite human nature in *Ethics* I and *Politics* I had taught. Thus King Charles I in 1642 could think of no better way to counter the Long Parliament's demands for enlarged powers than to conclude his *Answer to the XIX Propositions* by repeating the celebrated words of the assembled barons of the Merton parliament of 1236: *Nolumus Leges Angliae mutare,* We do not want the Laws of England to change![10] And James Otis, in 1764, appealed beyond the recently established convention of absolute parliamentary sovereignty to the unchanging natural and divine order in this striking language:

To say Parliament is absolute and arbitrary is a contradiction. The Parliament cannot make 2 and 2, 5: omnipotency cannot do it. The supreme power in a state is *jus dicere* [to speak law] only: *jus dare* [to give or make law], strictly speaking, belongs alone to God. Parliaments are in all cases to *declare* what is for the good of the whole; but it is not the *declaration* of Parliament that makes it so.

There must be in every instance a higher authority, viz., GOD. Should an act of Parliament be against any of *his* natural laws, which are *immutably* true, *their* declaration would be contrary to eternal truth, equity, and justice, and consequently void. . . . All power is of GOD. Next and only subordinate to Him in the present state of the well formed, beautifully constructed British monarchy. . . , [whose] pillars are fixed in judgment, righteousness, and truth, is the King and Parliament.[11]

It is difficult to imagine a more perfectly medieval view of human law in its relationship to natural and eternal law than Otis's statement.[12] The point to stress for the moment, however, is that this sentiment infused the restorative thrust of the Revolution; for what was to be restored was the reasonable and just ordering of human affairs so as to harmonize again human and divine governance in natural concord. Nor was this solely or even primarily a matter of secular or civil concern. To the contrary, ecclesiastical polity and religious liberty were equally at issue. The strength of Americans' reaction against obnoxious trade regulations and taxes, tending (they were convinced) toward the enslavement of freemen, was powerfully magnified by the growing conviction that the very terms upon which salvation itself depended were, for each of them, profoundly jeopardized by a comprehensive conspiracy against liberty:

Too much emphasis cannot be laid on the fact that sooner or later there was something in British policy that directly affected, or seemed to threaten, the religious or political liberties of every individual in the English colonies. Each successive step toward further commercial and political control by authority external to the colonial assemblies was apparently accompanied by parallel proposals to extend ecclesiastical control. This almost rhythmic or periodic sequence of external regulations and piling up of events during the sixties induced a situation that was highly charged with emotion. . . . The sustained secular drift of our own times must not be permitted through sheer ignorance or cynicism to black out of history the potent fact that religion was the central concern for most Americans, not only throughout the entire century and a half of settlement on this continent but of the era of the Revolution as well. Who can deny that for them the very core of existence was their relation to God?. . . No less eminent personage than the [great evangelist] George Whitefield gravely warned two prominent ministers at Portsmouth, New Hampshire, in April 1764: "There is a deep laid plot against both your civil and religious liberties, and they will be lost. Your golden days are at an end." When the Grenville reform program took effect in 1764 and 1765, many colonials had come to the conclusion that the Sugar, Currency, and Stamp acts and the plan for [an Anglican] bishop were all part of one concerted plan. . . . John Adams . . . urged all printers to spread news of this imminent catastrophe throughout the land. Obviously he accepted the idea of a conspiracy to subvert American liberties and sought to link civil and religious tyranny in the minds of his readers.[13]

The repeal of the Stamp Act in March 1766 was immediately followed by enactment of the Declaratory Act in which Parliament asserted its right to bind the colonies "in all cases whatsoever." The cry of "Tyranny!" that then went up, beginning with James Otis's "black regiment, the dissenting clergy" and his committees of correspondence, thundered through America in a steady crescendo to climax in Independence and Tom Paine's *Crisis Papers* a decade later.[14] Published in the deep gloom of retreat the day before Washington's famous crossing of the Delaware on Christmas Eve, 1776, *Crisis* I captured the somber resolve and pathos of the Revolution in these bitter words:

Britain, with an army to enforce her tyranny, has declared that she has a right (not only to TAX) but "to bind *us in* ALL CASES WHATSOEVER," and if being *bound in that manner*, is not slavery, then is there not such a thing as slavery upon earth. Even the expression is impious; for so unlimited a power can belong only to God. . . . Not all the treasures of the world . . . could have induced me to support an offensive war, for I think it murder; but if a thief breaks into my house, burns and destroys my property, and kills or threatens to kill me, or those that are in it, and to *"bind me in all cases whatsoever"* to his absolute will, am I to suffer it? What signifies it to me, whether he who does it is a king or a common man; my countryman or not my countryman; whether it be done by an individual villain, or any army of them? . . . Let them call me rebel and welcome, I feel no concern from it; but I should suffer the misery of devils, were I to make a whore of my soul by swearing allegiance to one whose character is that of a sottish, stupid, stubborn, worthless, brutish man.[15]

The paradigm of Revolution itself, then, was conceived similarly to *stasis* in Aristotle, but with biblical overtones added. Outrage over property matters and unconscionable injustice lay at the root of American discontent. The perversion (*parekbasis*) of the monarchy admired by Otis into the tyranny loathed by Paine at the hands of George III, the ministry and their parliamentary accomplices, aroused the sense of injustice in the citizenry to the point where stability finally gave way and the people withdrew allegiance from a king who had wantonly violated his trust. There was no question of tyrannicide, however. The Lockean "appeal to Heaven" might be cited, and indeed it was. But the whole of medieval Christian constitutional and political theory as well lay squarely behind the American determination. The pungency of Paine's words in *Crisis I* arises partly from the skill with which he brings to bear the older elements of the political heritage in concert with the newer elements supplied by the contract theorists. From William the Conqueror onward, the English community was founded on *fides,* first symbolized in ceremonies of liege homage and the oath of fealty in a reciprocal act of faith between man and Lord in which service and allegiance were promised in return for protection, peace, and justice. The mutual bonds of obligation so covenanted were cemented by the pledge of one's Christianity itself; or as Pollock and Maitland stated it, "he pawn[ed] his hope of salvation."[16] If either party failed to meet his obligations, then the other was freed from his. The essentials of this relationship were retained into modern times and symbolized in the English coronation ritual.

The teaching of St. Thomas also is apposite, not as the voice of the "popish" church roundly despised by most of our revolutionaries as the reign of the Antichrist overthrown at the Reformation, but as a great spokesman of the medieval Christian synthesis.[17] For St. Thomas, "just as the government of a king is the best, so the government of a tyrant is the worst."[18] The end of rule befitting freemen is the common good of the multitude. Such rule is right and just when it conduces to the happiness of men, their natural and eternal end. Such is kingly rule, or true rule, whether by one, a few, or the many. Perverse rule, of which the worst is tyranny in its absolute form, on the other hand, does not aim at the common good but at the private good of the ruler(s) and is, therefore, unjust.[19] The tyrant, more specifically, is one who "oppresses by might instead of ruling by justice."[20] How can a people rid themselves of a tyrant? Among other alternatives, St. Thomas offers these:

If to provide itself with a king belongs to the right of a given multitude, it is not unjust that the king be deposed or have his power restricted by that same multitude if, becoming a tyrant, he abuses the royal power. It must not be thought that such a multitude is acting unfaithfully in deposing the tyrant, even though it had previously subjected itself to him in perpetuity, because he himself has deserved that the covenant with his subjects should not be kept, since, in ruling the multitude, he did not act faithfully as the office of king demands. . . . Should no human aid whatsoever against a tyrant be forthcoming, recourse must be had to God, the King of all, who is a helper in due time in tribulation. . . . But to deserve to secure this benefit from God, the people must desist from sin, for it is by divine permission that wicked men receive power to rule as a punishment for sin. . . . Sin must therefore be done away with in order that the scourge of tyrants may cease.[21]

And, finally, St. Thomas counsels in this vein: "Man is bound to obey secular princes in so far as this is required by the order of justice. Wherefore if the prince's authority is not just but usurped, or if he commands what is unjust, his subjects are not bound to obey him. . . ."[22] The drift of St. Thomas's words closely accords with the logic of the American revolutionaries (however vehemently they might have scorned the association), as the pathos of national days of "publick humiliation" and all that went with it eloquently suggests. Moreover, the Declaration's persuasive dynamic echoes the common heritage of classical and Christian civilization shared by the thirteenth-century philosopher and our eighteenth-century Founders. For that document's initial and final appeals to God and the natural order of reason and justice for ultimate justification bracket a bill of particulars wherein "absolute Tyranny" is proved against George III. So far from securing peace, protection, and justice essential to the common good of his people, "He has abdicated Government here, by declaring us out of his Protection and waging War against us." In so doing, monarchy has been perverted into tyranny, with the justifiable and necessary consequences that faith is broken and obligations covenanted between king and people dissolved: ". . .the good People of these Colonies . . . are Absolved from all Allegiance to the British Crown, and . . . all political connection between them and the State of Great Britain . . . is and ought to be totally dissolved. . . ."[23] In brief, the action is to depose the monarch because he has become a tyrant, and

to declare independence for the reconstituted community and its
new polities, the States. The guiding sentiment of the action was
perhaps best captured by the motto Jefferson chose in 1776 for his
personal seal: "Rebellion to tyrants is obedience to God."[24]

Jefferson claimed he looked at no books in drafting the Declaration: "All of its authority rests then on the harmonizing sentiments
of the day, whether expressed in conversation, in letters, printed
essays, or in the elementary books of public right, as Aristotle,
Cicero, Locke, Sidney, etc., &c."[25] The classical, as well as feudal,
cast of Jefferson's thinking is underscored by his language of the
time as used elsewhere, and it sustains the account of the meaning
of the Declaration in certain of its key aspects just summarized.
The "Composition Draft" of the Declaration containing the charges
against the King was substantially identical with Jefferson's drafts
for the pertinent part of the Virginia Constitution of 1776. It
opened with these words: "Whereas George Guelph King of Great
Britain & Ireland and Elector of Hanover, heretofore entrusted
with the exercise of the Kingly office in this government, hath
endeavored to pervert the same into a detestable & insupportable
tyranny [:] 1. by putting his negative on laws the most wholesome
& necessary for the public good. . . . 16. and finally by abandoning
the helm of government & declaring us out of his allegiance & protection."[26] In his "First Draft" of the Virginia Constitution, Jefferson wrote that "public liberty may be more certainly secured by
abolishing an office which all experience hath shewn to be in-
veterately inimical thereto, and it will thereupon become further
necessary to re-establish such antient principles as are friendly to
the rights of the people. . . ." A later passage continues: ". . . it is
declared that the said colonies are in a state of open Rebellion &
hostility against the king & his parliament of Great Britain, that
they are out of their allegiance to him & are thereby also put out of
his protection. . . ." Whereupon Jefferson quotes from "the original
charter of compact granted [by Queen Elizabeth] to Sr. Walter
Raleigh on behalf of himself & the settlers of this colony & bearing
date the 25th of March 1584" whose terms supply justification for
"lawfully, rightfully, & by consent of both parties divest[ing George
Guelf] of the kingly powers."[27] In the "Second Draft": ". . . he is
hereby deposed from the kingly office within ys. government & absolutely divested of all it's [sic] rights & powers. . . ."[28] In the
"Third Draft": because of his "misrule George Guelf has forfeited

the kingly office and has rendered it necessary for the preservation of the people that he should be immediately deposed from the same. . . ."[29]

A king who perverts his rule is a tyrant. He perverts it by abandoning public good in favor of using his power against the people for private good, that is for the good of only a part of the community. For this the people can justly depose him, *if* it is within their purview to provide themselves a king. We have seen that these were thoroughly medieval Christian notions, with roots in the teachings of Aristotle and St. Thomas. But they were equally American conceptions by 1776. What of the missing links? Did the king's authority rest on the people's consent? As early as 1765 John Adams delivered this warning to the English in reacting to the abusive policies of Grenville and his henchmen: "Do you not represent [the king and parliament] as forgetting that the prince of Orange was created King William [III in 1689], *by the people,* on purpose that their rights might be eternal and inviolable?"[30] Aristotle's teaching plainly undergirds Adams's caustic reminder of the English constitution's principles: "[K]ingship implies government with consent as well as sovereignty over the greater part of affairs . . . for when subjects cease to consent, a king is no more a king; but a tyrant is still a tyrant, though his subjects do not want him."[31]

To depose the King clearly lay within the right of the people. But on what specific terms? In the unfolding debate over American rights and the place of the colonies in the British empire, arguments were conducted on a variety of levels, political theory and natural rights perhaps being the ones most attended to by scholars. Obviously, however, the constitutional debate was central historically, and within that the questions of authority and allegiance were pivotal. This brings to view the feudal relationship between America and the English monarchy within the empire. For from 1773 onward, in rejecting the authority of Parliament to legislate for them (to bind them "in all cases whatsoever," as the unrepealed Declaratory Act of 1766 obnoxiously and alarmingly asserted), the Americans turned to the king. Led by the Boston Adamses, Sam and John, they argued that personal allegiance to the king in the reciprocal bonds of protection, homage, and fealty constituted the *sole* bond of community with England. John Adams's scathing denunciation of the feudal system and its covert popery of 1765 did not prevent his shifting the debate to the new

ground by 1774. Earlier, Adams had derided bitterly the notion of
the personal relationship between mother and child which the court
claimed underlay the detestable policies of Great Britain toward
the colonies. It reminded him (with "horror") of Shakespeare's
depiction of another mother, Lady Macbeth, who

> 'Had given suck, and knew
> How tender't was to love the babe that
> milked her,
> but yet, who could
> Even while't was smiling in her face
> Have plucked her nipple from the boneless gums,
> And dashed the brains out.'[32]

In the *Resolutions* adopted by the First Continental Congress on
October 14, 1774, Adams prevailed over the stubborn opposition of
Joseph Galloway to win approval of this familiar language:

> That the foundation of English liberty, and of all free government, is
> a right in the people to participate in their legislative council; and as
> the English colonists are not represented, and from their local and
> other circumstances, cannot properly be represented in the British
> parliament, they are entitled to a free and exclusive power of legisla-
> tion in their several provincial legislatures, where their right of
> representation can alone be preserved, in all cases of taxation and
> internal polity, subject only to the negative of their sovereign, in such
> manner as has been heretofore used and accustomed.

In their petition to the king adopted on October 26, Congress called
England "that nation" with which the Americans are in contention
and stated: "We wish not a diminution of the prerogative."[33]

The basis of this final and rather astonishing constitutional position of the Americans lay in reasoning elaborated at length in
Adams's *Novanglus* and succinctly displayed in a Massachusetts
document of 1773; and the position taken there rested, in turn,
primarily on the precedent of *Calvin's Case*, decided in 1608. By the
feudal basis of the relation of realm to dominions, lordship and
dominion are solely in the king, all power is his; feudal principles
"afford us no idea of parliament." Considered as merely feudatory,
"we are subject to the king's absolute will, and there is no authority
of parliament, as the sovereign authority of the British empire."
Moreover, no allegiance is due by Americans to "the crown of

England." The tie is a strictly *personal* one: "Every man swears allegiance for himself, to his own king, in his natural person." Coke's opinion in *Calvin's Case* is quoted: " 'Every subject is presumed by law to be sworn to the king, which is to his natural person. The allegiance is due to his natural body.' . . . If, then, the homage and allegiance is not to the body politic of the king, then it is not to him as the head, or any part of that legislative authority. . ." vested in Parliament. Rather, "our ancestors received the lands [in America], by grant, from the king; and, at the same time, compacted with him, and promised him homage and allegiance, not in his public or politic, but natural capacity only." It then follows that "the right of being governed by laws, which were made by persons in whose election they had a voice, [our ancestors] looked upon as the foundation of English liberties. By the compact with the king, in charter, they were to be free in America as they would have been if they had remained within the realm; and, therefore, they freely asserted that they 'were to be governed by laws made by themselves, and by officers chosen by themselves.' " To hold otherwise and subject Massachusetts' people to the arbitrary will of a Parliament in which they have no voice, one claiming authority to make laws binding upon them in all cases whatsoever "without our consent," can only be "destructive of the first law of society, the good of the whole."[34]

This feudal conception of the English constitution is distinctly contrary to the Whig principle – whether New Whig or Old Whig – of vesting sovereignty in Parliament. In plain fact, this is the medieval conception of the English constitution. It supplemented the appeal to natural law and rights in the late phases of the debate leading to Independence. And it alone makes intelligible both Jefferson's designation of the king as "George Guelph" and the stress placed in both the Virginia Constitution and the Declaration of Independence as adopted on proving the political sins of the monarch, with only minimal attention being paid Parliament. The personal relationship was central, the bonds of faith reciprocal between persons in America and the person of the king; the king had broken his faith in perverting just rule into misrule, thereby freeing the Americans from their obligation of allegiance. Parliament's role in this scenario was constitutionally negligible (whatever its actions), since by the Americans' theory it had no valid claim whatever to authority over them.

It is worthwhile to give the last word to John Adams in this
rather technical argument, although the testimony of Benjamin
Franklin, James Wilson, John Dickinson, and Thomas Jefferson
might also be adduced. In *Novanglus* he summed up the cardinal
point this way:

> Lands are holden according to the original notices of feuds, of the
> natural person of the lord. Holding lands in feudal language, means
> no more than the relation between lord and tenant. The reciprocal
> duties of these are all personal. Homage, fealty &c. and all other ser-
> vices, are personal to the lord; protection, &c. is personal to the ten-
> ant. And therefore no homage, fealty, or other services, can ever be
> rendered to the body politic, the political capacity, which is not cor-
> porated, but only a frame in the mind, an idea. No lands here, or in
> England, are held of the crown, meaning by it the political capacity;
> they are all held of the royal person, the natural person of the
> king. . . . as soon as [the colonists] arrived here, they got out of the
> English realm, dominions, state, empire, call it by what name you
> will, and out of the legal jurisdiction of parliament.[35]

General Perspective and a Quibble or Two

IT IS, OF COURSE, no novelty to point out that Christianity is basic
to American politics. This has been done before by many writers in
many ways, few more incisively than Tocqueville, who published
this view in 1840:

> It was religion that gave birth to the English colonies in America.
> One must never forget that. In the United States religion is mingled
> with all the national customs and all those feelings which the word
> fatherland evokes. For that reason it has peculiar power. . . . Chris-
> tianity has kept a strong hold over the minds of Americans, and . . .
> its power is not just that of a philosophy which has been examined
> and accepted, but that of a religion believed in without
> discussion. . . . Christianity itself is an established and irresistible
> fact which no one seeks to attack or to defend.[36]

Ralph Barton Perry, over a century later, reported that America is
a "Christian country" whose "general Hebraic-Christian-Biblical
tradition embraces ideas so familiar that, like the air, they are in-
haled without effort or attention."[37] And he identified the "fallacy
of difference" in the delineation of Puritanism by writers who un-
warrantably ignore the fundamentally common ground shared by

Puritans with all other Christian communions – a point of consideration for an argument that cites Thomas Aquinas in viewing the American Revolution as a study in restoration. "Puritanism was an offshoot from the main stem of Christian belief, and Puritans, equally with Catholics, claimed descent from St. Paul and Augustine. . . ." Puritanism he defines as "theocractic, congregational-presbyterian, Calvinistic, protestant, medieval Christianity."[38] Persuasive scholarship has traced the rise of *Americanism* itself to the Great Awakening of the 1720s onward as the beginning of a series of waves of revivalism rising and falling down to the end of the eighteenth century and even beyond. This surge of renewed faith can be seen as the decisive factor in the emergence of American national consciousness by the 1760s. The Great Awakening, Herbert Osgood flatly states, "was an event of general human significance" marking an "epoch" in our history.[39]

The citations might go endlessly on. The curiosity is that relatively little detailed connection with political theory has been traced after the decline of Puritanism toward the end of the seventeenth century. The influence of the classical philosophers is minimized even more, despite the fact that one can scarcely read a paragraph of the political literature of the revolutionary period without stumbling on direct classical allusions and steady use of the Greek and Roman categories of thought. In his exciting analysis, Bernard Bailyn identifies at the outset five major sources of revolutionary thought, including classical antiquity and New England Puritanism: the former he decides is universal, but merely illustrative rather than determinative of thought; the latter is important for the covenant theology, the contribution of the notion of the cosmic, providential sweep of America's destiny, ubiquitous, but ultimately incoherent and filled with conflicts. Enlightenment thought is directly influential, but superficial apart from Locke, who is centrally important; and the common law is historically important but not determinative. Dominant and determinative for our revolutionaries, Bailyn finds, is the "radical social and political thought of the English Civil War and Commonwealth period"; Milton, Harrington, and especially Sidney composed the "textbook of the Revolution." It is this strand of thinking, Bailyn contends, which drew together and harmonized all other elements into the distinctive synthesis seen in the formative period.[40]

I have here time to say only that in so concluding, I think Bailyn wrong, even if elegantly wrong. Christianity and classical theory together constitute the matrix of both the sense of community and the "antient principles" of man and government whose synthesis distinguishes the Founders' thought. This synthesis they and I call by the familiar name Americanism. McIlwain was close to the fact when he asserted that "1768 was the high-water mark of Whiggism in America. There it stopped."[41] Alan Heimert, his Harvard colleague, once remarked of Bailyn that he wrote almost as though the preachers did not exist. While too much need not be made of a casual observation, there is indeed in Bailyn's account a suspicion of what Perry Miller called "obtuse secularism." As to the mobilizing sentiment of the American Revolution, Miller added: "A pure rationalism such as [Jefferson's] might have declared the independence of these folk, but could never have inspired them to fight for it."[42] Neither Louis Hartz's "irrational Lockianism," nor Wills's or others' Enlightenment thought, nor Bailyn's Country ideology deserves first regard in our understanding of the mind of the American Founders—significant as all three may be in the sophisticated and highly stratified consciousness of that uncommonly well educated generation.[43]

The meaning of equality and happiness as held by such *aristoi* as Jefferson and Adams, and the esteem in which the *people* are held in the repeated references to them in the Constitutional Convention, are quite mystifying unless the classical and Christian notions of a common human nature present to all men *qua* men and the dignity of man as created in the divine image and loved of God are borne in mind.[44] As John Adams asserted in 1765:

A native of America who cannot read and write is as rare an appearance as a Jacobite or a Roman Catholic, that is, as rare as a comet or an earthquake. It has been observed that we are all of us lawyers, divines, politicians, and philosophers. . . . [A]ll candid foreigners who have passed through this country, and conversed freely with all sorts of people here, will allow, that they have never seen so much knowledge and civility among the common people in any part of the world. . . . Be it remembered . . . that liberty must at all hazards be supported. We have a right to it, derived from our Maker. But if we had not, our fathers have earned and bought it for us, at the expense of their ease, their estates, their pleasure, and their blood. And liberty cannot be preserved without a general knowledge among the people, who have a right, from the frame of their nature, to knowledge, as their great Creator, who does nothing in vain, has given them understanding, and a desire to know. . . .[45]

Constitutional and Historical Perspectives: Conclusion

TIME AND SPACE available here permit no more than a passing glance at the constitutional and historical perspectives commonplace to the Founders. But I can scarcely conclude without stressing a few of the central points. Richard Gummere is indubitably right in his judgment: "The delegates to the Constitutional Convention assembled at a time when the influence of the classics was at its height. They were not interested in mere window dressing or in popular slogans filched from history books. They dealt with fundamental ideas and considered them in light of their applicability."[46] Aristotle, Cicero, and Polybius were central. The majority of delegates to the Convention knew the classics, as Gummere shows and as one can conclude easily enough for himself by reading through the character sketches of fifty-three of the participants done by William Pierce of Georgia in the Convention.[47]

The central principle of the Constitution, as establishing a rule of law and not of men, took its rise from Aristotle's *Politics,* book III, chapter 16, as did also the fundamental insight into human nature of that passage that Madison and his colleagues institutionalized in the separation of powers and system of checks and balances – expounded in *Federalist No. 47-51* – as Edward Corwin knew a half-century ago:

"To invest the law then with authority is, it seems, to invest God and reason; to invest a man is to introduce a beast, as desire is something bestial, and even the best of men in authority are liable to be corrupted by passion. We may conclude then that the law is reason without passion and it is therefore preferable to any individual. . . ." The opposition which [Aristotle's formulation] discovers between the desire of the human governor and the reason of the law lies, indeed, at the foundation of the American interpretation of the doctrine of the separation of powers and so of the entire system of constitutional law.[48]

The mediation of common notions of rule from antiquity by such important writers as Harrington, Bolingbroke, Montesquieu, and others ought not confuse the fact that the original sources were

Greeks and Romans; and the Framers knew not only the mediators but the originators themselves, thoroughly and often in the original languages. Madison's repeated clarification of the "ends" of man and government as happiness and justice, and the echoing agreement with him on all sides, trace to the headwaters of Plato and Aristotle as confirmed in Cicero and Polybius. Toward the close of *Federalist No. 51*, Madison's summary is clear: "Justice is the end of government. It is the end of civil society. It ever has been and ever will be pursued until it be obtained, or until liberty be lost in the pursuit." After opening the *Ethics* with the clarification that the highest good attainable by action is Happiness, Aristotle went on to his analytical inquiry, arriving at this pertinent juncture:

> The laws make pronouncements on every sphere of life, and their aim is to secure . . . the common good of all. . . . Accordingly, in one sense we call those things "just" which produce and preserve happiness for the social and political community.[49]

To be sure, the Founders kept the context of their efforts constantly in mind in fashioning the Constitution, an attitude strongly present also in Plato's *Laws* and Aristotle's *Politics* for all of the amplitude of their vision of transcendental truth. As Pierce Butler of Georgia phrased the Framers' task: "We must follow the example of Solon who gave the Athenians not the best Gov't. he could devise; but the best they wd. receive." And above all that meant, as Gouveneur Morris said much later in the Convention's proceedings, to remember that, in America, "The people are king."[50] Still, the *Justice* to which the Constitution was dedicated was that of the higher Law of God and Reason – the "Law coeval with mankind" in Cicero's phrase, as Blackstone had reaffirmed for the hundredth time in 1765, when volume one of the *Commentaries* appeared.[51] In short, it is divine and natural Justice which supplies the standard of what is lawful and within the reach of the consent of the people by their Constitution.

The historical vista is accordingly wide. The sobriety of Americans in politics also characterizes their view of history and the nation's destiny. Apocalypticism is a potent factor from the early years of settlement onward, but I think it was never a dominant one. Still, there is the understanding of special favor and an intimacy with God that supplies peculiar meaning to America's pilgrimage through time. Americans, for all their enthusiasm in religion from time to time, could never forget the fundamental of the faith: "My kingdom is not of this world." But at the Founding, the New Order of the Ages was, in fact, proclaimed; and Manifest Destiny appeared before the eighteenth century was out. And if the end of history and the translation of time into eternity at the millennium are eagerly anticipated, along with America's special role in this final fruition of faith, then the representative attitude is suspenseful and hopeful rather than dogmatic and certain. The flavor is caught by the illustrious Ezra Stiles in his Election Day sermon of 1783, in a passage with which I close:

> I have thus far shown wherein consists the true political welfare of a civil community or sovereignty. The foundation is laid in a judicious distribution of property, and in a good system of polity and jurisprudence, on which will arise, under a truly patriotic, upright, and firm administration the beautiful superstructure of a well-governed and prosperous empire. . . . Already does the new constellation of the United States begin to realize . . . glory. . . . And we have reason to hope, and I believe, to expect that God has still greater blessings in store for this vine which his own right hand hath planted, to make us high among the nations in praise, and in name, and in honor. The reasons are very numerous, weighty, and conclusive.[52]

Notes

[1] William James, *A Pluralistic Universe* in *Essays in Radical Empiricism: A Pluralistic Universe,* ed. Ralph Barton Perry (1942; repr. ed., Gloucester, Mass.: Peter Smith, 1967), 2:263.

[2] Thomas Jefferson to Edward Rutledge, June 24, 1797, *Writings of Thomas Jefferson,* ed. A.A. Lipscomb and A.E. Bergh, 20 vols. in 10 (Washington, D.C.: Thomas Jefferson Memorial Association, 1905), 9:409. For "Americanism" in Adams, *Old Family Letters: Copies from the originals for Alexander Biddle* (Philadelphia, 1892), p. 70.

[3] For the theories of articulation and representation implicit here, see Eric Voegelin, *The New Science of Politics: An Introduction* (Chicago: University of Chicago Press, 1952), chaps. 1-3.

⁴ J.G.A. Pocock, *The Machiavellian Moment: Florentine Political Thought and the Atlantic Republican Tradition* (Princeton: Princeton University Press, 1975), p. 462.

⁵ The period indicated is from James Otis's speech against the writs of assistance of February, 1761, to the ratification of the Bill of Rights in December, 1791, the beginning and end of the Revolution.

⁶ The phrase "great rights of mankind" is Madison's, taken from his speech on June 8, 1789, in the House of Representatives, in which he introduced the Bill of Rights for adoption as amendments to the Constitution. Quotes from Bernard Schwartz, ed., *The Bill of Rights: A Documentary History*, 2 vols. (New York: Chelsea House Pubs., McGraw-Hill Book Co., 1971), 2:1024.

⁷ Perry Miller, "From Covenant to Revival," in *Religion in American Life*, ed. J.W. Smith and A.L. Jamison, 4 vols. (Princeton: Princeton University Press, 1961), 1:325.

⁸ *Ibid.*, p. 322.

⁹ *Ibid.*, pp. 326, 361.

¹⁰ Cf. Corinne Comstock Weston, "Beginnings of the Classical Theory of the English Constitution," *Proceedings of the American Philosophical Society* 100 (April, 1956): 133-44 at 144.

¹¹ James Otis, "The Rights of the British Colonies Asserted and Proved," in *Pamphlets of the American Revolution, 1750-1776*, ed. Bernard Bailyn, 4 vols. (Cambridge, Mass.: Belknap Press, 1965), 1:454, 456. Emphasis as in the original.

¹² Cf. St. Thomas Aquinas, *Summa Theologica* I-II. 90-97.

¹³ Carl Bridenbaugh, *The Spirit of '76: The Growth of American Patriotism Before Independence, 1607-1776* (London, Oxford, New York: Oxford University Press, 1975), pp. 117-19.

¹⁴ *Ibid.*, pp. 120-21.

¹⁵ Philip S. Foner, ed., *The Complete Writings of Thomas Paine*, 2 vols. (New York: Citadel Press, 1945), 1:50, 55. Emphasis as in original.

¹⁶ F. Pollock and F.W. Maitland, *The History of English Law Before the Time of Edward I*, 2nd ed., 2 vols. (Cambridge: At the University Press, [1898]), 2:190. Cf. Sandoz, "Political Obligation and the Brutish In Man," *Review of Politics* 33 (Jan. 1971): 95-121 at 103-104.

¹⁷ Cf. Ernest L. Tuveson, *Redeemer Nation: The Idea of America's Millennial Role* (Chicago: University of Chicago Press, 1968), pp. 17-19 and *passim*. This view of Reformation and papacy is not uniquely American, of course. For example, for the *Pope as Antichrist* by Melchior Lorch see the plate, as well as the general analysis, in Norman Cohn, *The Pursuit of the Millennium: Revolutionary messianism in medieval and Reformation Europe and its bearing on modern totalitarian movements*, 2nd ed. (New York: Harper & Brothers, Torchbook, 1961), facing p. 48 and *passim*.

[18] St. Thomas Aquinas, *On Kingship* I. 3.21.

[19] *Ibid.,* I. 1.10.

[20] *Ibid.,* 11.

[21] *Ibid.,* I. 4.49, 51, 52; quoted from Dino Bigongiari, ed., *The Political Ideas of St. Thomas Aquinas: Representative Selections* (New York: Hafner Pub. Co., 1969), pp. 190-92.

[22] *Summa Theologica* II-II. 104. 6, reply obj. 3.

[23] Quotations from the Declaration are from *Documents Illustrative of the Formation of the Union of American States,* 69th Congress, 1st Session, House Document no. 398 (Washington: Government Printing Office, 1927), pp. 24-25.

[24] Julian P. Boyd, ed., *Papers of Thomas Jefferson,* 19 vols. to date (Princeton: Princeton University Press, 1950-), 1:677-79. Boyd's conclusion here is that Benjamin Franklin probably originated the motto.

[25] Paul L. Ford, ed., *Writings of Thomas Jefferson,* 10 vols. (New York: 1892-99), 10:343. The statement is hooted at by Garry Wills, *Inventing America: Jefferson's Declaration of Independence* (New York: Vintage Books, 1979), p. 174: recommending John Locke's *Second Treatise* to another, despite Jefferson's own supposed ignorance of the text himself, says Wills, was no more "dishonest" than ". . . his crediting Aristotle (of all people) with formation of the background for his Declaration." Wills's argument aims to disabuse us of the traditional and "useful vagueness of Jefferson" by proving him to have been specifically or "quintessentially a man of the Enlightenment; he lived in the world of Catherine and Diderot" (*ibid.,* p. 368). But Jefferson lived in some other worlds as well. Wills's argument is tendentious, whatever the merits of his book otherwise.

[26] Boyd, ed., *Papers of Thomas Jefferson,* 1:427,419. Cf. the wording of the Virginia Constitution (adopted June 29, 1776) in *ibid.,* pp. 377-78. For true and perverse rule and their relation to the common good, see Aristotle, *Politics* III. 7.

[27] Quoted from *Papers of Thomas Jefferson,* 1:339-40. Boyd dates this and the other two drafts "Before 13 June 1776."

[28] *Ibid.,* p. 347.

[29] *Ibid.,* p. 357.

[30] "Dissertation on the Canon and Feudal Law," in Charles F. Adams, ed., *Works of John Adams: Second President of the United States,* 10 vols. (Boston: Charles C. Little & James Brown, 1851), 3:447-64 at 461. Emphasis added.

[31] Aristotle, *Politics* V. 10; trans. T.A. Sinclair (Baltimore: Penguin Books, 1962), p. 224.

[32] Adams, "Dissertation on the Canon and Feudal Law," *Works of John Adams* 3:461. For the shift in Adams's emphasis, see *Novanglus* in *ibid.,* 4:1-177, which fully explores the feudal-medieval theory of the English con-

stitution as sketched herein.

[33] Quoted from Charles H. McIlwain, *The American Revolution: A Constitutional Interpretation* (New York: Macmillan Co., 1923), pp. 114-16.

[34] Quoted and summarized from *ibid.*, pp. 130-36; cf. pp. 92-95 for the details of *Calvin's Case.*

[35] *Works of John Adams*, 4:176-77. Cf. McIlwain, *The American Revolution*, pp. 138-47. The views stated by Adams were voiced already by Franklin in 1766; *ibid.*, p. 147.

[36] Alexis de Tocqueville, *Democracy in America*, ed. J.P. Mayer, trans. George Lawrence, 2 vols. in 1 (Garden City, N.Y.: Doubleday & Co., Inc., Anchor Books, 1969), p. 432. Volume one of *Democracy in America* appeared in 1835, the second volume (from which the quotation is taken) in 1840.

[37] Perry, *Characteristically American* (New York: A.A. Knopf, 1949), p. 93.

[38] Perry, *Puritanism and Democracy* (New York: Vanguard, 1944), pp. 82-83.

[39] Herbert L. Osgood, *The American Colonies in the Eighteenth Century*, 4 vols. (1924; repr. ed., Gloucester, Mass.: Peter Smith, 1958), 3:409. Carl Bridenbaugh confirms the judgment in numerous places, *e.g. Cities in Revolt: Urban Life in America, 1743-1776* (New York: A.A. Knopf, 1955), pp. 64, 150-56, 424.

[40] Bernard Bailyn, *Ideological Origins of the American Revolution* (Cambridge: Belknap Press, Harvard University Press, 1967), pp. 23-35, 53.

[41] McIlwain, *The American Revolution*, p. 157.

[42] Miller, *Religion in American Life*, eds. Smith and Jamison, 1:336n, 343. For Heimert's settled views, see his *Religion and the American Mind: From the Great Awakening to the Revolution* (Cambridge: Harvard University Press, 1966).

[43] See Louis Hartz, *The Liberal Tradition in America* (New York: Harcourt, Brace & World, Inc., Harvest Books, 1955), p. 62 and *passim.*

[44] For the discussion of *aristoi* (best men by nature) see *The Adams-Jefferson Letters. . . ,* ed. Lester J. Cappon, 2 vols. in 1 (1959; repr. ed., New York: Simon & Schuster, Clarion Books, 1971), pp. 387-92, Jefferson's letter dated Oct. 28, 1813; also the other letters in this period, *ibid.,* pp. 365-99.

[45] *Works of John Adams*, 3:456. Cf. Aristotle, *Metaphysics* I, first line: "All men by nature desire to know."

[46] Richard M. Gummere, *The American Colonial Mind and the Classical Tradition: Essays in Comparative Culture* (Cambridge: Harvard University Press, 1963), p. 174; for the college curriculum and its thorough education of Americans in the classics, pp. 55-59.

[47] *Ibid.,* p. 178. Cf. "Notes of William Pierce (Ga.) in the Federal Conven-

tion of 1787," in *Documents Illustrative of the Formation of the Union*, pp. 96-108.

[48] Corwin, *The "Higher Law" Background of American Constitutional Law* (1928, 1929; repr. ed., Ithaca, N.Y.: Cornell University Press, Great Seal Books, 1955), pp. 8-9.

[49] Aristotle, *Nicomachean Ethics* V.1; trans. Martin Ostwald (Indianapolis, New York: Bobbs-Merrill, Library of the Liberal Arts, 1962), p. 113.

[50] "Debates in the Federal Convention of 1787 as Reported by James Madison," in *Documents Illustrative of the Formation of the Union*, pp. 159, 421.

[51] Cicero, *Republic* III.33; *Laws* I.18. William Blackstone, *Commentaries on the Laws of England*, 1:41.

[52] Ezra Stiles, "The United States Elevated to Glory and Honor," in *The Pulpit of the American Revolution. . . ,* ed. John W. Thornton (Boston: Gould and Lincoln, 1860), pp. 438-39. An edited version of this sermon is reprinted in Conrad Cherry, ed., *God's New Israel: Religious Interpretations of American Destiny,* (Englewood Cliffs, N.J.: Prentice-Hall, 1971), pp. 82-92, which also contains useful bibliographies. For analysis, see Tuveson, *Redeemer Nation.*

Bibliographic Note: I have made no attempt to reconcile the argument of this essay with the substantial body of scholarly debate most closely related to it, particularly as that addresses the question of the Founders' debt to classical political theory. In that regard, see especially the following: Gordon S. Wood, *The Creation of the American Republic* (Chapel Hill, N.C.: University of North Carolina Press, 1969); Gerald Stourzh, *Alexander Hamilton and the Idea of Republican Government* (Stanford, Calif.: Stanford University Press, 1970); and the assessment of Wood's and Stourzh's arguments, together with the literature cited, in Pocock, *The Machiavellian Moment*, pp. 506-52 (cf. Note 4, above), Juergen Gebhardt, *Die Krise des Amerikanismus: Revoluntionaere Ordnung und gesellschaftliches Selbstverstaendnis in der amerikanischen Republik* (Stuttgart: Ernst Klett Verlag, 1976), pp. 116-47 and *passim*, and Gary J. Schmitt and Robert H. Webking, "Revolutionaries, Anti-Federalists, and Federalists: Comments on Gordon Wood's Understanding of the American Founding," *Political Science Reviewer* 9 (1979): 195-229.

Christianity, Ideology,
and Political Philosophy

Paul Sigmund

WHEN VOLTAIRE EXCLAIMED "Écrasez l'infâme," he expressed a
sentiment typical of the French Enlightenment's attitudes to
Christianity. Indeed, as Peter Gay has argued, the one common element in the diverse group of Enlightenment thinkers was their
hostility to Christianity.[1] Going further, one can even argue that
opposition to organized Christianity has been a common
characteristic of most of the great writers in the Western political
tradition since the Renaissance – Machiavelli, Hobbes, Locke
(against Roman Catholicism), Rousseau, Bentham, Marx, and Mill.
Since its foundation in fifth century Greece by a Socrates who was
put to death for impiety, political philosophy has frequently, implicitly or explicitly, challenged the claim of religion to be a source
of political norms, and asserted the prior claim of "reason" to
establish the foundations of legitimacy and the political order.
More recently, sociologists since the time of Max Weber and
modernization theorists such as Alex Inkeles and David Apter have
described the advance of secularization as an inevitable and
desirable consequence of modernity. Even theologians writing in
the sixties seemed to celebrate "the Death of God," the demise of
traditional religion, and hailed the advent of the "Secular City" in
which a theology of social change became the principal burden of
the Christian message.[2]

Yet at a time when there appears to be a revival of religious
awareness everywhere from the college campuses of the United
States to the streets of Teheran, it is difficult to argue the in-

evitability of the triumph of secularism. Moreover, one of the ironies of the history of philosophy is that the same Age of Enlightenment that attacked the claims of religion to be the sole source of moral and political norms, also produced in the philosophy of David Hume (his famous analysis in the *Treatise of Human Nature* of the impossibility of deriving evaluative statements from factual ones) a powerful critique of the derivation of such norms from reason. As many – but not all – contemporary democratic theorists retreat into relativism or skepticism, the claim of Christianity to provide an ultimate source of the values upon which political philosophy rests once more merits re-examination – if only because the claims of reason to provide such norms have been seen as either epistemologically dubious, logically untenable, or psychologically unpersuasive as the ground of political commitment.[3]

Yet does the Christian message carry a specific political content? Has it not been used – and misused – by so many regimes and societies as to demonstrate that it is capable of application in support of just about any government or political system or attitude? Does not Christ's very statement, "My kingdom is not of this world" (John 18:36), indicate a lack of concern with political institutions and structures? To answer these questions we must take a closer look at the basic documents that contain the message of Christ – the New Testament – and then attempt to evaluate the way that that message has been, or can be, applied to the political order.

II

The New Testament attitude toward politics is an ambivalent one – part of a larger ambivalence toward "this world." This ambivalence is a consequence of the conflicting conclusions that can be drawn from the doctrines of Creation, the Fall, and Redemption. The world is the result of an act of creative will by a beneficent God, but it has also been corrupted by the deliberate turning away from God by man, and reconciled with Him through the coming of His Son. It thus can neither be totally rejected nor totally accepted. While there have been those in Christianity, as in other religions, who have withdrawn from the sin and corruption of the world to pursue spiritual perfection, Christianity's founder did not do so. Although, as we now know, there were monastic communities such as Qumran and ascetic sects such as the Essenes in contemporary Judaism, there is no evidence that Jesus was a member of any of these. He mingled with worldly people – tax collectors and prostitutes – and saw his mission as directed to all – including those not accepted by the Jews of his time, such as the Samaritans and Gentiles.

On the other hand, Christ seems clearly to have refused direct political involvement. The New Testament record indicates that he rejected an invitation to become a nationalist leader (John 6:15); refused the temptation to exercise worldly rule (Matt. 4:9); accepted the payment of taxes to the Roman occupiers when many of his contemporaries did not (Matt. 22:21); and repeatedly emphasized that he was preaching the Kingdom of Heaven, not an earthly kingdom. Personal repentance for sin, not political liberation, was his message, and the recognition by Christians that the world and the political order are flawed as a consequence of sin must temper any attempt to identify one or another political structure or activity with the message of salvation.

The New Testament message was not completely irrelevant to politics, however. When the Gospels were interpreted by some as releasing Christians from their political and social obligations, Paul wrote "Let every soul be subject to higher powers. . . . The powers that be are ordained of God. Whosoever resisteth the power, resisteth the ordinance of God" (Romans 13:1-2), and Peter urged Christians to obey the king, and slaves to be subject to their masters (Peter 2:17-18). On the other hand, Christians also refused, as a matter of religious principle, to participate in the worship of the emperor, and when the apostles were arrested and forbidden to preach, Peter replied, "we must obey God rather than man" (Acts 5:29). Christianity both supported the political status quo and challenged it. It did so because the New Testament now provided a different standard to judge and to limit political institutions – the will of a transcendent God who was not identified with any particular political entity or authority, but was Himself the source and measure of authority. Politics became relativized. In contrast to the Greek view of political life as the fulfillment of man's highest potential, politics for the Christian was at best only a means to a higher end, and political involvement merely one of a number of ways in which the individual could work out his or her salvation.

A further consequence of the coming of Christianity was that a new form of organized community was established, based on conversion, an act of the will, rather than on tradition or ascription, and characterized by authority structures of its own – which in the first centuries of Christianity and down to the present day included elements of all three classic forms of government: monarchy (the papacy), aristocracy (the episcopate), and democracy (the Christian community). The classical problem of the best form of government was set in a new context with a standard of evaluation which was both old and new – the will of God; but the arguments over the structure of authority in the Church were couched in terms of political theory, as well as of God's will, and had important implications for the development of political as well as ecclesiastical thinking.[4]

Besides the structural and theological aspects of the New Testament which had political implications, there are two more specifically doctrinal elements in Christianity which should be mentioned – Christ's attitude toward violence, and his suspicion of economic affluence. On the first point, Christ is very explicit. Love of God and neighbor are the whole of the Law (Mark 12:30). Christians must turn the other cheek, love their enemies, and do good to those who hate them (Matt. 5:39-44), but those who live by the sword will perish by it (Matt. 26:52). (The single exception – one that has given support to Christian exegetes who argue that some uses of violence may be legitimate – is the incident in which Christ used whips to drive the money-changers from the temple [John 2:15]). The implications of the Christian doctrine of love in a violent world must continue to concern those who wish to apply Christ's doctrine to political life.

On the question of the negative spiritual affects of the possession of worldly wealth, Christ is again very explicit. If one is to be perfect, he or she must sell his possessions and give the proceeds to the poor (Mark 10:21). Whatever may be the correct translation of the reference to the camel and the eye of the needle (Mark 10:25), it is clear that the rich have little chance of attaining heaven. Lazarus, the poor leper, is taken up into Abraham's bosom while the rich man is condemned to hell (Luke 16:19-26). It is obedience to God's word, not "bread alone," material well-being, that should be the goal of human action (Matt. 4:4). God puts down the mighty, fills the hungry with good things and sends the rich away empty

(Luke 1:52-53).

We may conclude this section then by arguing, in summary, that the New Testament provides an ultimate standard for judging and limiting any political order or philosophy, commands the Christian to work out his salvation in a world created by God but flawed by sin, and opposes violence and worldly wealth. What are the implications of these conclusions for political philosophy?

III

I do not want to get into the various controversies concerning the meaning of the term "ideology." I intend to use it, first, in the sense of an all-embracing world view that provides a social group with a standard of value and a guide to action. If it is defined in this sense, I think that it is clear from what I have said above what the Christian attitude should be. No ideology is entitled to claim total commitment, and any view of this world must inevitably be qualified by the Christian's belief in his eternal destiny and obedience to God's will as to how he should attain it. This does not mean that he cannot be committed to an ideology, but only that the commitment must always be qualified by a higher loyalty and goal – and if a political ideology becomes a species of secular religion in its demand for total commitment, the Christian is precluded from embracing it.

On the other hand, if ideology is defined in a narrower sense as a shared view of politics – a political philosophy held in common with others – it is clear that any Christian who is involved in political life, or even thinks about it at all, will possess, explicitly or implicitly, a set of political values that could be described as ideological in a narrow sense. "Every little boy and girl alive" may not be forced to choose between being "liberal or conservative," but citizens in modern societies are compelled to make political decisions, and in doing so they usually reveal certain consistent value preferences which may be placed along the left-right spectrum that has been familiar to us since the French Revolution. If we look at the historical experience of Christianity in the modern period, we find that Christians as well as non-Christians have tended to group themselves at three particular points along that spectrum which we can identify respectively as conservative, liberal, and radical.

Christians, however, possessing a different ultimate standard of judgment, have tended to identify and justify their political affilia-

tion in religiously based terms. And I would argue that if that identification is not totalistic, if the moral and theological limits of
political commitment are observed, there are good reasons for such
political involvement in Christian doctrine and tradition. All three
of the basic ideological/philosophical political positions can be
justified from, and based upon, Christian premises–but none
should be completely identified with Christ's message.

(a) Conservative writers are suspicious of attempts to produce
rapid social, economic, and political change, and respect institutions which have a lengthy historical existence. They usually
believe in the immutability of certain basic moral values, and are
skeptical of the possibilities of carrying out major changes by
political or governmental action. American conservatism also sup-
ports economic freedom and individual rights, while it is dubious
about the possibilities of creating a moral order in international
relations. All of these positions can be, and have been, justified
from a Christian point of view. Catholic, Anglican, and Orthodox
Christians have religious reasons for reverencing tradition, and
ascribe importance to ecclesiastical institutions as a medium for
the transmission and development of the Christian message. The
doctrine of an absolute morality based on natural law and natural
rights is rooted in a Christian world view (*e.g.,* in the writings of
Aquinas, Hooker, as well as Locke, to a degree not acknowledged
by many of his interpreters). The hierarchical world view described
in Lovejoy's book, *The Great Chain of Being,* was based on a blend
of Christianity and neo-Platonism which dominated the West down
to the seventeenth century.[5] The attacks on liberalism by the
nineteenth-century papacy were conservative responses to anti-
clerical governments in France and Italy, and more recently the so-
called "labor encyclicals" of Leo XIII and Pius XI were an attempt
to develop a religious justification for a modern version of medieval
corporatism, which could provide an alternative to both in-
dividualistic capitalism and collectivist socialism. Pius XI's doctrine
of "subsidiarity," supporting and encouraging the development of
intermediate institutions between the individual and the
state–especially, of course, those under church sponsorship–is
also one that many conservatives would endorse.

Historically, however, there have been some problems with the
type of Christian conservatism just described. The first is that
Christian conservatives sometimes tended to insist that conser-

vatism is the only political outlook that a believing Christian could embrace, and to use the instruments of state power to assure that this was the case – whether through a religious establishment, persecution of or discrimination against non-believers, or, in democratic politics, church endorsement of conservative parties. The second problem has been the frequent inability of Christian conservatives to distinguish between a genuine conservatism which respects the limits of political activity and state control, and a fascism, state corporatism, or integralism which is fundamentally opposed to the values in which true conservatives believe (*e.g.*, Franco's falangism in Spain, the corporatism of Mussolini, Brazilian integralism in the thirties, and the attempts of the Pinochet regime in Chile in September 1973 and March 1974 to make use of Catholic social doctrines to justify the 1973 coup and the repression that followed). An additional problem – to which we will return later – is the difficulty that Christ's strictures on the use of violence and on concentrations of economic power pose for conservatives' readiness to support the use of force in international relations, and their opposition to labor and welfare legislation.

(b) Like conservatism, liberalism is capable of many different interpretations. However, its core values of individual liberty – whether promoted by the welfare state or by laissez-faire democracy – and constitutionally protected rights, have often been derived from Christian assumptions. In the Anglo-American tradition, the Puritan and Quaker contributions to the theory and practice of liberty are well known, and a paper has been presented at this conference on the Christian origins of American political thought. European and Latin American Catholicism at first saw liberalism as inimical to its doctrines, but more recently philosophers such as Jacques Maritain and the leaders of the Christian Democratic parties on both continents have grounded their beliefs in democracy and human rights on a Christian view of man. Christian trade unionism has asserted the rights of the working man, and official Catholic teaching since World War II, especially since the papacy of John XXIII, has endorsed basic liberal tenets in the name of Christian values, even going so far as to defend the nationalization of some basic industries (*Mater et Magistra*, 1961) and a right to freedom of worship (*Pacem in Terris*, 1963, and Vatican II's *Declaration on Religious Freedom*, 1965) in terms that seemed quite opposed to earlier official papal statements.

Liberalism, however, is not without its problems for the Christian. In its laissez-faire version, it asserts an absolute (or rather, quasi-absolute, because even laissez-faire theory admits the right of taxation for security and police purposes) right to property and an economic individualism that is difficult to reconcile with Christian social obligations and with Christ's criticisms of wealth. Social welfare liberalism runs the risk of excessive expansion of state power, and in the specific case of state-financed abortions, promotes what in the opinion of many Christians is the taking of innocent life. Relativist versions of liberalism contradict Christian belief in the existence of moral absolutes, while at the other extreme, doctrinaire liberals have opposed the right of the church to carry out educational and charitable activities with public support. In addition, while not as ready as conservatives to support the use of violence to suppress crime and aggression, liberals have on the whole been reluctant to exclude it in the more extreme situations, sometimes opposing capital punishment, for instance, but usually accepting government spending for defense and domestic and international security.

(c) Christianity and political radicalism would seem to have little in common. Yet there is no lack of historical examples of Christian willingness to attempt the establishment of "a new heaven and a new earth" (Revelation 21:1). Eric Voegelin has identified this tendency with the Gnostic heresy and has seen the three-state theory of history of the medieval mystic, Joachim of Flora, as the intellectual progenitor of this type of chiliastic Christian radicalism.[6] In the modern period, one can see the whole range of ideological responses among the various Christian sects during the English Civil Wars, and more recent examples of left-wing Christianity include the nineteenth-century abolitionists, some Christian participants in the anti-war movement in the United States in the 1960s, and the proponents of the theology of liberation in Latin America. In each case, radical demands are rooted in Christian perceptions of human equality, pacifism, or social justice, which reject any compromise with social or political expediency.[7]

Support for radical and violent revolution would seem to be difficult to reconcile with the Christian doctrine of love. Yet it must be admitted that the use of violence in defense of justice has been justified by Christians throughout recorded history. Christian conservatives have endorsed the persecution of heretics and defended holy wars and crusades, while the just war doctrine has been given both liberal and conservative interpretations by Christian writers. The new Christian defenders of revolutionary violence either expand some of the already existing categories used by traditional theologians arguing for a right of self-defense against "institutionalized violence," or condemn the dualism and other-worldliness of earlier approaches to the relation of religion and politics.[8]

More often the radical interpretation of Christ's message in this area takes a pacifist form, and rejects on religious grounds the use of violence (at least, when it results in killing of other human beings) in favor of absolute non-resistance or non-violent forms of opposition to the status quo. As noted earlier, there are clear pacifist strains in the Christian message, and it has been so interpreted in recent centuries by the Peace Churches such as the Quakers, the Mennonites, and the Brethren. Yet most Christians have been willing to accept the legitimacy of the use of coercion by duly constituted authority, whether parental, judicial, military, or political. Christian writers from St. Augustine to Reinhold Niebuhr have argued that in a sinful world it is not possible to establish the Kingdom of God on earth based on love and absolute non-resistance; at the same time they have placed serious limits upon the exercise of violence – so serious that a number of writers now doubt that modern warfare, at least in its nuclear form, can ever be justified.[9]

Another strain of Christian radicalism focuses on the interpretation of the Christian message that emphasizes social justice and commitment to the poor. We have already cited Christ's strong criticism of the wealthy and his concern for the poor. In recent years this has been interpreted as implying a commitment to oppose exploitation, economic inequality, and, particularly in Latin America, the capitalist system as a whole. There have always been anti-capitalist elements in Christianity – especially in the Catholic tradition – but in the past they have ususally taken a conservative or even reactionary form: longing for the order, stability, and hierarchy of an earlier age that has been disrupted by the economic and political changes associated with the spread of capitalism. What is new, particularly in Latin America, is the attempt to link a religious critique of capitalism with the endorsement of socialism as the uniquely Christian economic system. This in turn leads to a debate on violence and non-violence and the conditions in which revolution is justifiable on Christian grounds.

What is lacking in much of this discussion is a vision of how the new Christian socialism would operate, although some of the Christian experiments in economic democracy in Spain, Chile, and Peru are of interest in this respect. Conversely, a defense of capitalism has rarely been undertaken on moral or religious grounds – along the lines, for example, of John Rawls, who argues in *A Theory of Justice* for the possibility of the moral justification of economic inequality if it improves the lot of all those involved, especially the least advantaged.[10]

A further failing of the Christian radicals has certain parallels on the left with the conservative blindness toward extremists on the right. Christian radicals striving to overcome economic injustice are often unwilling to admit that other radical groups, attempting to achieve the same goals, may be committed to philosophies and political systems that are basically hostile to religious values and human freedom. This has been particularly true in recent years as religious energies have been directed less at opposing atheism and totalitarian regimes, and more at combating racism, exploitation, and (Western) militarism – all areas in which Marxists have been particularly active in the West and in the Third World.

IV

What are we to conclude from the examination of the variety of political philosophies and ideologies that have been, and can be, derived from Christian premises? One possibility is to refer to the possibility of the Devil's use of biblical quotations, and conclude that the quest for Christian political philosophy is a vain one. As the analysis above indicates, however, my own view would be a less pessimistic one. While it is an illusion – and indeed opposed to the message of Christ – to identify a particular political view as *the* Christian political theory, we can, as I hope I have demonstrated, identify several different and indeed conflicting political views as capable of being supported by Christian doctrine and practice. The choice between them depends on arguments which are differently grounded but structurally similar to those made by the non-Christian political thinker. Certain values such as order and hierarchy, liberty and participation, equality and the end of exploitation, are derived from Christ's message and made the basis for one's preferred political system and practice. Those values, however, should be held and applied by the Christian in ways that avoid the fanaticism and absolutism that, regrettably, have often characterized both religiously-based politics and the quasi-religions of the great modern secular ideologies, for "we have not here a lasting city" and Christ's kingdom is not of this world. Extreme solutions of the left and right (or for that matter, the doctrinaire liberalism of the center) are excluded, for the Christian knows that, as Aquinas said, "Man is not ordained in all that he is and has to the political community . . . but to God."[11]

The continuing problem for a Christian political theory is to analyze and develop the most ambiguous and politically charged elements in Christ's message: how Christ's command to love God and neighbor is to be applied to the control of violence and the promotion of justice for the poor. Conservatives, liberals, and radicals disagree fundamentally about how this should be done–but those who are Christians cannot deny that they have a religious duty to do so. In areas where Christian culture is still strong (the American South and South Africa in the case of Protestantism, southern Europe and Latin America in the case of Catholicism, and even in more secularized areas of Western Europe and North America) there is still an important role for the political theorist and practitioner in bringing Christian insights, historically conditioned and fallible as they may be, to bear upon the solution of political problems–while recognizing that their final resolution, however, remains in the hands of the Creator.

Notes

[1] Peter Gay, *The Enlightenment: an Interpretation* (New York: Alfred A. Knopf, 1966).

[2] Gabriel Vahanian, *The Death of God* (New York: George Braziller, 1961); Harvey Cox, *The Secular City* (New York: Macmillan, 1965).

[3] See David Hume, *A Treatise of Human Nature*, bk. III, pt. 1, chaps. 1-2; T.D. Weldon, *The Vocabulary of Politics* (Baltimore: Penguin Books, 1953); Arnold Brecht, *Political Theory* (Princeton: Princeton University Press,

1959); Giovanni Sartori, *Democratic Theory* (New York: Praeger, 1965); Felix Oppenheim, *Moral Principles in Political Thought* (New York: Random House, 1968). For an anti-relativist approach, see John H. Hallowell, *The Moral Foundations of Democracy* (Chicago: University of Chicago Press, 1954).

[4] See my argument in *Nicholas of Cusa and Medieval Political Thought* (Cambridge: Harvard University Press, 1963), concerning the impact of the conciliar controversy on the development of Western political theory.

[5] Arthur O. Lovejoy, *The Great Chain of Being* (Cambridge: Harvard University Press, 1936). On Christianity and natural law, see my *Natural Law in Political Thought* (Cambridge: Winthrop Publishers, 1971; repr. Washington, D.C.: University Press of America, 1981).

[6] Eric Voegelin, *The New Science of Politics* (Chicago: University of Chicago Press, 1952). See also the criticism of Voegelin from a Christian point of view in Frederick D. Wilhelmsen, *Christianity and Political Philosophy* (Athens: University of Georgia Press, 1978), chap. 7.

[7] On the English sects see, for example, William Haller, *Liberty and Reformation in the Puritan Revolution* (New York: Columbia University Press, 1955); Michael Walzer, *The Revolution of the Saints* (Cambridge: Harvard University Press, 1965); as well as the numerous books on the subject by Christopher Hill. On contemporary Christian radicalism, see John C. Bennett, *The Radical Imperative* (Philadelphia: The Westminster Press, 1975); Gustavo Gutierrez, *Theology of Liberation* (Maryknoll, N.Y.: Orbis Books, 1973); and my article "Latin American Catholicism's Opening to the Left," *Review of Politics* 35 (January, 1973): 61-76. See also Jeremy Rivken, *Entropy* (New York: Viking Press, 1980), for an attempt to link environmentalist anti-capitalism to Christian notions of man's "stewardship" of nature.

[8] See, for example, the statement of the Golconda Group in Colombia translated in Paul E. Sigmund, *The Ideologies of the Developing Nations* (New York: Praeger, 1972), pp. 466-468. On Christianity and Marxism, see Arthur McGovern, *Marxism, an American Christian Perspective* (Maryknoll, N.Y.: Orbis Books, 1980).

[9] See Roland Bainton, *Christian Attitudes towards Peace and War* (Nashville, Tenn.: Abingdon Press, 1960); Paul Ramsey, *War and the Christian Conscience* (Durham, N.C.: Duke University Press, 1961) and *The Just War* (New York: Scribners, 1968); John C. Bennett, ed., *Nuclear Weapons and the Conflict of Conscience* (New York: Scribners, 1961); Albert Marrin, ed., *War and the Christian Conscience* (Chicago: Regnery, 1971); John H. Yoder, *The Politics of Jesus* (Grand Rapids: William B. Eerdmans, 1972); the documents in Donald F. Durnbaugh, ed., *On Earth Peace* (Elgin, Ill.: Brethren Press, 1978); and *The Challenge of Peace: God's Promise and Our Response, A Pastoral Letter on War and Peace* (Washington, D.C.: National Conference of Catholic Bishops, 1983). See

also the controversy elicited by S.G.F. Brandon, *Jesus and the Zealots* (Manchester: University of Manchester Press, 1967), especially Oscar Cullmann, *Jesus and the Revolutionaries* (New York: Harper and Row, 1971).

[10] John Rawls, *A Theory of Justice* (Cambridge: Harvard University Press, 1971), chap. 2. For a recent attempt to provide a moral and religious justification for capitalism, see Michael Novak, *The Spirit of Democratic Capitalism* (New York: Simon and Schuster, 1982).

[11] St. Thomas Aquinas, *Summa Theologiae*, I-II. 21. 4.

Political Theory:
The Place of Christianity

James V. Schall, S.J.

IN AN ESSAY on "Teaching History to the Rising Generation," Russell Kirk told of the textbook his daughter was assigned in the sixth grade of a Roman Catholic grammar school. "In the whole of the textbook, there is no mention of Christianity or Christ, no mention of Catholicism or of any other Christian or Jewish persuasion. . . . One is left to conclude that none of (the) large (historical) themes has been influenced by religion in any way."[1] The question can also be asked quite naturally at a higher educational level and not only in a parochial environment: Is the treatment of Christianity much better at the university level, and this not merely in history departments? In particular, is the academic discipline of political theory, with its various conferences, journals, departments, and curricula, so designed in practice that it can be presented as if Christianity did not and does not exist? Anyone familiar with the field, no doubt, will suspect that the latter is largely the case. Christianity is not in practice seen to be connected with the core integrity of the discipline itself. At most, it is a marginal theoretic issue, of some importance in certain past eras, quite often with harmful results. There is, it would seem, some need to state the opposite position, at least for the sake of argument, namely, that political philosophy cannot be fully itself without understanding the relationship of Christianity to its premises and contents. The relative neglect of Christianity must, then, itself be accounted for.

"Too much politics, like too much education, is a sign of social decline," V.A. Demant wrote in his essay, "The Theology of Politics." "The temptation of the natural man is to seek one unifying principle short of God. This is sought in some immanent fact of the natural and historic process."[2] Politics remains the most natural and human substitute for God, since politics is, in its own right, a "unifying principle." This is why, intrinsic to itself, political theory requires a reason to be limited and *self*-limiting. The essential contribution of theology to political theory is, on this basis, philosophical. That is, by locating ultimate being outside of the legitimate tasks open to mankind to accomplish by its own efforts, theology at its best prevents political theory from becoming its own metaphysics, prevents it from being, again in Demant's words, "some immanent fact of the natural and historical process." For metaphysics, however it be called, is a discipline that presumes, on its own grounds, to account for all being – all natural and historical being, itself implicitly identified with *that which is*.[3] When this latter effort appears under the guise of political theory, it limits total reality to that which appears under the methodological processes available to the study of politics.

Without the transcendent, however, politics has no intrinsic limits, since in itself, it is, properly, the highest of the practical sciences, as both Aristotle and Aquinas held. Without a theoretic limit, politics naturally tends to become absolute, a discipline designed to place everything under its scope. On the other hand, an authentic political theory will be, even in its sense of its own reality, essentially "self"-limiting, to the extent it realizes that the whole of being and reality is *not* to be identified with that aspect of reality which is human, which deals with man as "the mortal," as Hannah Arendt used to say.[4] In this connection, then, we are able to suggest that to explore political theory is first to examine its natural and also extrinsic limits. The import of this position can clearly be sensed if we recall the traditional idea that theology was the "queen of the sciences." We should not, then, easily pass over what Professor Leo Strauss wrote at the beginning of his *The City and Man:*

> It is not sufficient for everyone to obey and to listen to the Divine Message of the City of Righteousness, the Faithful City. In order to propagate that message among the heathen, nay, in order to understand it as clearly and as fully as is humanly possible, one must consider to what extent man could discover the outlines of that City if left to himself, to the proper exercise of his own powers. But in our

age it is much less urgent to show that political philosophy is the indispensable handmaiden of theology than to show that political
philosophy is the rightful queen of the social sciences, the sciences of
man and of his affairs.[5]

Whether, some twenty years later, the urgency is still in the direction Professor Strauss suggested, can be questioned. But anyone
familiar with the central line of Western tradition will immediately
recognize in his reflections themes from Aristotle and Augustine,
Plato and Aquinas.

Yet, it is safe to say that few Christian thinkers have recognized
the enormous implications to theology contained in Leo Strauss's
monumental works.[6] For his subtle argument was to ask about the
limits of the "queen of the social sciences," political philosophy
itself, in order to allow a space for revelation or at least its possibility. He understood, in other words, that even on its own grounds,
political theory could not account for everything that guided and
influenced nature and man. Hence, in urging political philosophers
to "discover the outlines of that City if left" to themselves, Strauss
recognized that self-limitation was the natural consequence in a
discipline that was not itself a true metaphysics. This legitimated
the enterprise of political theory itself, with its own relative
autonomy – what the Christians called, "rendering to Caesar"
– while not requiring political philosophy to explain everything,
all that is, a task proper to man, even though not a political task.
This is why Aristotle said that even the little we could
know of the divine things was worth all our efforts, even though
politics was "proper" only to man.[7] In de-emphasizing the "handmaiden" relationship, Strauss evidently made a place for the same
function within the discipline of political philosophy itself, or at
least tried to do so.

Political theory, for its part, has also something very basic to say
to contemporary theology and religion. From the ordinary viewpoint of the political theorist, theology seems presently to state its
case before the world precisely in political terms and guises, yet
with few of the limits to which political reflection, at its best, is subjected. This makes theology seem more and more unreal, even
naive. It often advocates lethal policies in the name of "justice"
without ever even suspecting where political things actually go,
without ever having heard of the chapters in Plato and Aristotle on

the decline of states. Today, it is not the theologian who complains about the encroachment of politics. Rather, the political theorist, while surveying what is purported to be theological reflection, wonders if theology has anything at all to say other than the political, a political that seems but a determined image of contemporary ideology. The curricula of theology or religion departments and seminaries often vaguely parallel those of government departments, with little clear notion of any differences in content or procedure. From the viewpoint of academic political theory, then, the major encroachment today is not from the political to the theological, but (particularly in the area of economics and development and "rights," and in the founding and rule of the new and poorer nations) from the theological to the political. Theology almost seems to have admitted that politics is indeed an autonomous metaphysics, contrary to the tradition of Aristotle and Aquinas.[8] Today, there are priests who want to become politicians (even after the papal decree to the contrary).[9] In the Christian tradition, however, as in the case of Ambrose of Milan, it was the politicians who became bishops and priests. The hierarchy of value was reversed.

What political philosophy has to tell religion, then, is the grounded estimate, based on judgment, experience, and law, of what can be expected in terms of virtue and practice from the generality of mankind as each person exists in a given culture. Ironically, this is what religion used to tell politics, before religion began to claim for itself the advocacy of the ideal human good, as it has tended to do more and more in conformity with modern revolutionary utopias, especially Marxism.[10] To deny that men can always be "better" is, therefore, as "un-Christian" as to expect them actually to produce the Kingdom of God on earth.[11] "We can hardly measure what the modern doctrine of individualism must owe to the Christian belief that men are spiritual beings, born for eternity, and having a value incommensurate with anything else in the created universe," the great Protestant historian, Professor Herbert Butterfield, wrote in his essay on "Christianity and Politics."[12] But, as he went on to suggest, the doctrine of universal sin, with particular attention to one's own sinfulness, was designed "to be a serious check on the many evils and mistakes in politics." Likewise, G.K. Chesterton, in his still even more formidable *Orthodoxy*, found the political connected with this doctrine: "Christianity is the only thing left that has any real right to question the power of the well-nurtured or the well-bred. . . . If we wish to pull down the prosperous oppressor we cannot do it with the new doctrine of human perfectibility; we can only do it with the old doctrine of Original Sin."[13] Only if *all* men and women are sinners can we realize that our governments, composed as they likewise are of these same men and women, must be designed to prevent these same people who actually rule us, even with our own advice and consent, from also abusing us.

Thus, by itself, politics could not know how valuable each person really was. All it could do is to project, with a Professor Rawls, that we all must be important because we all would, with various veils of ignorance, project the same fate for ourselves. Yet, by itself, politics could neither know nor account for the depths of evil and disorder that are operative and somehow expected among men. The holocausts we describe and acknowledge do not prevent their repetition among us. They only guarantee that the destiny of the sufferers cannot be finally accounted for by politics alone. The saint, Aquinas remarked, is above the law, because he observes the law, knows it, whereas the politician must account for the majority of us who are not saints.[14] The politician who does not understand how men can abuse one another, who does not believe that holocaust is *possible,* is simultaneously a bad politician *and* a bad theologian. He does not know how to rule because he does not know what to expect.[15] Thus, when once the truth of the value of each person *and* his concrete sinfulness is comprehended, it becomes the legitimate task of politics to account for their realities within the political realm, to account for the absolute dignity of human beings and for the possibility of mass political destruction and the more frequent lesser evils.[16] This is why politics ultimately does have something to teach theology even about itself. For it is the politician who must confront men also in their sinfulness, however it be called, while leaving a real space for their virtue, a space that does not "coerce" a particular definition of goodness on men. The politician must seek a "common good" even among the less than perfect, the kind of people Aquinas held to be the primary objects of civil law.[17] The task of political theory, as Plato had already intimated in *The Republic,* the first book of the discipline, is to find a place for the Good that transcends the ordinary political experience of the normalcy of men. Specifically Christian political theory begins with the Incarnation, with Augustine's realization that the Good, happiness, was indeed a necessary aspect of human reflection and endeavor, but that its fullness was not proper to this world, not achievable by human, particularly political, means.

In his still perceptive essay, "St. Augustine and His Age," the Catholic historian Christopher Dawson pointed out why the reality of transcendence, the dignity of the person, and the persistence of evil and sin—each a foundation of politics and of what is *beyond* politics—can become the basis of a new kind of social order that results from the effect of the Christian stimulus in the world. "In the West, however," Dawson wrote, "St. Augustine broke decisively with this tradition by depriving the state of its aura of divinity and seeking the principle of social order in the human will. In this way, the Augustinian theory, for all its otherworldliness, first made possible the ideal of a social order resting upon the free personality and a common effort towards moral ends."[18] This idea that the social order was to be based upon the dignity of individual persons, who had the capacity to "will"—the philosophical discovery the late Professor Hannah Arendt in her *The Life of the Mind* attributed directly to Christianity— this capacity to direct human actions to moral or immoral ends even within the political order, seemed to make political theory free from any scientific determinism, even from sociology or psychology.[19] The "causes" of social disorder or progress, therefore, had to be located in the vices or virtues, in the various definitions men gave to the actual existential happiness which they individually sought, choices eventually reflected, as Aristotle knew in the First Book of his *Ethics,* in the forms of government described in *The Politics.*[20]

"Value-free" political theory, consequently, as Professor Strauss and Professor Voegelin were quick to note in famous studies, explained everything but politics and that which transcended it.[21] The late E.F. Schumacher, in his remarkable *A Guide for the Perplexed,* was thus mostly correct in his observation that "the modern experiment to live without religion has failed, and once we have understood this, we know what our 'post-modern' tasks really are."[22] The post-modern endeavor for political theory is, consequently, precisely the rediscovery of specifically Christian political theory, a theory which does not, when it is itself, allow politics to become effectively a secular religion or substitute metaphysics, as it has, in effect, tended to become in the recent past, particularly in academic political theory. This would, likewise, be a theory that does not allow theology to destroy the things of Caesar.

There is, then, rather much truth in the ironical remark of Father Robert Sokolowski, Professor of Philosophy at Catholic University, when he said: "Perhaps we can say Christians forget that justice is a reflection of the image of the good and not the good itself. It is curious that Christians look for the divine in social order at a time when the social order itself has so much of the inhuman in it."[23] The rapid legalization of what were properly called "vices" in classical natural law theory has made it more and more imperative that political theory retain its principled foothold in theology and metaphysics, in a source that would prevent it from completing Machiavelli's modern project of identifying absolutely what men do with what they ought to do. The public order is more than ever being arranged so that we be not allowed to state the "untruth" of the laws and practices we have enacted against the classical norms.

"To speak knowingly the truth, among prudent and dear men, about what is greatest and dear, is a thing that is safe and encouraging." Such penetrating words of Socrates in the Fifth Book of *The Republic* are, of course, very circumspect. For the number of "prudent and dear men," among whom Socrates felt himself to be discussing where political thought ultimately led, is indeed too few. When, however, this same truth is spoken among the multitudes, it can be quite dangerous, as Socrates himself soon was to find out. Realization of this very danger was the background of Professor Strauss's emphasis on "secret writing," about what he called "persecution and the art of writing."[24] The social sciences had to search their own limits because, if men suspected such limits led to or arose from revelation, they would, perhaps stubbornly, refuse the search for the truth. This is why it is no accident that both Paul VI, in the Vactican II document on Religious Liberty (1965), and John Paul II, in his Address to the United Nations (October 2, 1979), took special and careful pains, from the side of religion, to insist upon the obligation of each person in himself not merely to pursue but to accept the truth on its own grounds, even the truth of revelation if it persuades. Truth may indeed make us free, but, as Solzhenitsyn and Strauss knew, it may also lead to persecution and tyranny by its rejection. The truth of political theory, from the viewpoint of the truth of original sin, may indeed lead to what does happen in actual political experience, to persecution of the just and the honest *because* they are just and honest. Man, in other words, always retains will as well as intellect.

The suspicion that the truth of political theory was bound up with the truth of metaphysics and revelation, then, has been the guiding principle of Western political theory – Christian, Jewish, and Muslim – until the modern era, until what the textbooks call, from Machiavelli, "modern" political theory.[25] The modern theoretical project, however, the one that now normally dominates the discipline, is based upon the intellectual "autonomy" of political theory. This means that the discipline contains within itself not only an historical *canon*, as Professor Pocock called it (a baker's dozen of basic authors from Plato to Augustine to Hobbes, Locke, Rousseau, and Mill, through which political theory is understood) but also a methodology and independent ground which is self-explanatory and self-justifying.[26] The extreme position was meant to be something quite different from Aristotle's notion of a "practical science," as he developed it in the Sixth Book of *Ethics*. It is different because, for Aristotle, the ends of the practical sciences were found in the metaphysical order.[27] Man did not "make" himself to be man, as Aristotle said, so that politics presupposed what made man to be man. Man's relation to himself, in other words, was not primarily one of self-making, but of self-discovery. And we can, properly, only "discover" what we ourselves do not make. Political theory appears in most academic and scholarly programs as the "history" of political theory, even though Professor Strauss warned that political philosophy ought not to be confused with the *history* of political thought.[28] Usually, political theory will be divided into the following categories: classical Greek and Roman; Jewish-early Christian-Roman Empire; Feudal and Christian Medieval; Modern, and Twentieth Century. However, the same enterprise can be divided in another fashion, according to the themes of "The Great Political Thinkers." The narrative histories of Professor Sabine or the more recent work of Professor Sibley would fill in the gaps of practice and theory for the less than "great."[29]

A third approach not infrequently used would be the "isms" analysis, as, for example, that used by the late Professor Ebenstein.[30] Here, attention would be paid rather to a single doctrine or ideology with its contents and problems. We would find in such an approach treatments of capitalism, democracy, communism, nazism, fascism, socialism, nationalism, behaviorism, corporatism, authoritarianism, anarchism, internationalism, and, perhaps, "developmentism," in the various offshoots of Professor Rostow's now-famous pioneer thesis about the "five states" of economic growth.[31] Finally, not a few endeavors would like to exorcise altogether the "history" of political theory in order to replace it with some procedure subject to "verifiable," scientific tools. In this way, political theory would, presumably, declare its independence from the tyranny of the past, of revelation, of metaphysics, even of history.[32]

In recent years, in most academic programs and official political science journals and associations, even in professedly "Christian" universities, a distinct intellectual "silence" has existed about the content and philosophical import of Christianity in political thought and affairs. One need only to inquire of good undergraduate classes – it is little better in graduate classes – about the identity of the Good Samaritan or the precise meaning of the Incarnation, Original Sin or the "City of God," all the common fare of the West for centuries and centuries, to realize that the terms of shared discourse are no longer readily available in the general academic community.[33] Official political science journals will too often – there are exceptions – return essays on formal Christian political theory and its implications in the discipline with the polite suggestion that they would be more "fitting" perhaps for theological journals. (And, alas, the quality of political discourse in the theological journals is often appalling.) We no longer suspect that William of Ockham, for example, in his analysis of the divine freedom, might have had something to do with the absoluteness of later, more modern political theory.[34] We do not see why the denial of the divinity of Christ is related to salvific ethos in much modern ideology.[35]

This severing of political theory from religion and theology, this studied "reductionism," however, has unfortunately served to separate them at a moment when religion, under the curious aegis of "liberation theology," is gaining an unprecedented political influence.[36] One has only to glance at the average weekly religious magazine, Protestant or Catholic, or diocesan newspaper, to realize that the major drift is political.[37] Political theorists, for their part, find themselves ill-equipped to handle the political overtones of the murder of an archbishop in a Central American cathedral, or the elevation of a revolutionary priest to the Office of

Foreign Affairs, or why it is not "illiberal" for the Roman Pope to
exclude the clergy from politics in Brazil. Moreover, this self-
isolation of political theory, the result of its own modernist
methodology, is itself in part responsible for the radicalization of
theology. This latter discipline almost never receives the sobering
analysis that ought to come from political theory at its best about
what we might expect of men in the world.[38] Thus, when it comes
to politics, contemporary theologians too often are the successors
of the Dr. Price who so incensed Edmund Burke in his *Reflections
on the Revolution in France:* "It is somewhat remarkable that this
Reverend Divine should be so earnest for setting up new churches,
and so perfectly indifferent concerning the doctrine which may be
taught in them."[39] Today's divines are equally earnest, though not
equally unconcerned about the direction of the doctrines they
espouse. Today, they are concerned not with setting up new
churches, but new governments and nations. Rendering to Caesar
has become, paradoxically, a clerical occupation, or at least a
clerical ambition, as the cynics have always suspected it would.

Ironically, then, the classical roles are almost reversed, so that
religion lacks the "realism" once expected of it, that source of sen-
sibility Reinhold Niebuhr once found in Augustine.[40] The doctrine
of the Fall did have political consequences in the very areas of property, coercive government, and labor, areas so related to modern
theory and ideology.[41] Political theory, on the other hand, appears
unable to articulate a coherent version of man or common good
that would permit "the political" to be less than a substitute
metaphysics, as it has become implicitly in so much contemporary
theory. This would seem to suggest that, even for its own health,
political theory must have addressed to it certain basic ideas and
religious affirmations that would force and convince politics to
limit itself to its own proper sphere.[42] Likewise, religion will not
long remain balanced if the experience of politics is not included as
a basic element in the analysis of how religion impacts on the
world, how human dignity is to be defended. The very nature of
man's intellect does, in classical reflection, give him a real source
for political knowledge.[43] "It may be accepting a miracle to believe
in free will," G.K. Chesterton wrote in *The Well and the Shallows,*

> ... but it is accepting madness, sooner or later, to disbelieve it. It
> may be a wild risk to take a vow, but it is quiet, crawling and in-
> evitable ruin to refuse to make a vow. It may be incredible that one

creed is the truth and others are relatively false; but it is not only incredible, but also intolerable, that there is no truth either in or out of creeds, and, all are equally false.[44]

The "miracles," "the wild risks," and the "incredibilities," which arise from a Western tradition that includes both faith and reason, seem those innovations that allow us to keep our politics sane and sensible.[45]

This, ultimately, is why Christianity cannot be avoided, along with the Old Testament, in the study of political theory; why religion needs to acknowledge that Caesar is to be rendered unto, within limits, to be sure.[46] This is why, too, the most remarkable part of Christ's famous distinction was not that God was before Caesar, but that Caesar did have a place by right. In limiting politics, Christianity limited religion.[47] Christian political theory is the intellectual limitation of the political by removing from Caesar what is not his. In Aristotelian terms, this leaves the "highest of the practical sciences," the "queen of the social sciences," to be what it is. The "Divine Message of the City of Righteousness, the Faithful City," then, ought to be sought, even listened to by political theory, for that is part of its discovery of itself. This is the place of Christianity in political theory, and the place of political theory in Christianity.

Notes

[1] Russell Kirk, *Educational Update* (Winter, 1980).

[2] V.A. Demant, *Theology of Society* (London: Faber, 1947), p. 218.

[3] J.M. Bochenski, *Philosophy: an Introduction* (New York: Harper, 1972).

[4] Hannah Arendt, *The Human Condition* (New York: Doubleday Anchor, 1959), p. 19.

[5] Leo Strauss, *The City and Man* (Chicago: University of Chicago Press, 1964), p. 1.

[6] Cf. James Steintrager, "Political Philosophy, Political Theology, and Morality," *The Thomist* 32 (July, 1968); Charles N.R. McCoy, *The Structure of Political Thought* (New York: McGraw-Hill, 1963); David Lowenthal, "The Case for Teleology," *The Independent Journal of Philosophy* 2 (1978).

[7] Aristotle, *Metaphysics* 981b25-983b29; *Nicomachean Ethics* 11412a31.

[8] Schall, "The Recovery of Metaphysics," *Divinitas* 2 (1979).

[9] Address of January 28, 1979.

[10] Cf. Roger Heckel, *The Theme of Liberation* (Rome: Pontifical Commission on Justice and Peace, 1980).

[11] Cf. Schall, "From 'Catholic Social Doctrine' to the 'Kingdom of God' on Earth," *Communio* 3 (Winter, 1976).

[12] *Herbert Butterfield: Writings on Christianity and History* (Oxford: Oxford University Press, 1979), p. 44.

[13] G.K. Chesterton, *Orthodoxy* (New York: Doubleday Image, 1908), pp. 116, 141.

[14] St. Thomas Aquinas, *Summa Theologica* I-II. 96.2; 96.5.

[15] Cf. Jeane Kirkpatrick, "Dictatorships and Double Standards," *Commentary* 31 (November, 1979).

[16] Cf. Schall, "Displacing Damnation: On the Neglect of Hell in Political Theory," *The Thomist* (January, 1980).

[17] Aquinas, *op. cit.* I-II. 96.2.

[18] Christopher Dawson, "Saint Augustine and His Age" in M.C D'Arcy, ed., *St. Augustine* (New York: Meridian Books, 1957), p. 77; cf. also John East, "The Political Relevance of St. Augustine," *Modern Age* 16 (Spring, 1972); Herbert Deane, *The Political and Social Ideas of St. Augustine* (New York: Columbia University Press, 1963).

[19] Arendt, *The Life of the Mind* (New York: Harcourt, 1978), vol. 2, *Willing;* Vernon Bourke, *Will in Western Thought* (Chicago: Sheed and Ward, 1955).

[20] Cf. Schall, "The Best Form of Government," *The Review of Politics* 40 (January, 1978).

[21] See Strauss, *Natural Right and History* (Chicago: University of Chicago Press, 1950); Eric Voegelin, *The New Science of Politics* (Chicago: University of Chicago Press, 1952).

[22] E.F. Schumacher, *A Guide for the Perplexed* (New York: Harper Colophon, 1977), p. 139.

[23] Robert Sokolowski, "Letter to the Author," 1979.

[24] Strauss, *Persecution and the Art of Writing* (Glencoe, Ill.: Free Press, 1952).

[25] Ralph Lerner and Muhsin Mahdi, *Medieval Political Philosophy* (Ithaca: Cornell University Press, 1972); Strauss, *Thoughts on Machiavelli* (Chicago: Free Press, 1958); McCoy.

[26] J. G. A. Pocock, *Politics, Language, and Time* (New York: Atheneum, 1973), pp. 5-15.

[27] McCoy, pp. 29-60; E. B. F. Midgley, "Concerning the Modernist Subversion of Political Philosophy," *The New Scholasticism* 53 (Spring, 1979).

[28] Strauss, *City*, p. 8; Pocock; Robert Dahl, *Modern Political Analysis*

(Englewood Cliffs, N.J.: Prentice-Hall, 1976).

[29] Cf. George Sabine, *A History of Political Theory* (New York: Holt, Rinehart & Winston, 1963); M. Mulford Sibley, *Political Ideas and Ideologies* (New York: Harper & Row, 1970); Michael Foster, *Masters of Political Thought* (Boston: Houghton-Mifflin, 1957); William Y. Elliot and Neil McDonald, *Western Political Heritage* (Englewood Cliffs, N.J.: Prentice-Hall, 1957); Lee McDonald, *Western Political Theory* (New York: Harcourt, 1968).

[30] William Ebenstein, *Today's Isms* (Englewood Cliffs, N.J.: Prentice-Hall, 1973).

[31] W.W. Rostow, *The Stages of Economic Growth* (London: Cambridge University Press, 1960).

[32] Cf. Heinz Eulau, *The Behavioral Persuasion in Politics* (New York: Random House, 1963).

[33] Cf. Schall, "On the Teaching of Ancient and Medieval Political Theory," *Modern Age* 19 (Spring, 1975). (Also in Schall, *Christianity and Politics* [Boston: St. Paul Editions, 1981], chap. 2.)

[34] Cf. Josef Pieper, *Scholasticism* (New York: McGraw-Hill, 1964).

[35] Cf. Stanislaw Fracz, "Neomarxistisches Jesusbild," *Stimmen der Zeit* 198 (Marz, 1980).

[36] Cf. Michael Dodson, "Prophetic Politics and Political Theory in Latin America," *Polity* 12 (Spring, 1980); cf. also Michael Novak, *The Theology of Democratic Capitalism* (New York: Simon and Schuster, 1982); Schall, *Liberation Theology* (San Francisco: Ignatius Press, 1982).

[37] Cf. E.O. Norman, *Christianity and the World Order* (New York: Oxford University Press, 1979) Jacques Ellul, *The Betrayal of the West* (New York: Seabury Press, 1978); Ernest Lefever, *Amsterdam to Nairobi: The World Council of Churches and the Third World* (Washington: Ethics and Public Policy Center, 1978); James Hitchcock, *Catholicism and Modernity* (New York: Seabury Press, 1979); Hitchcock, "A Church at Sea," *National Review* 35 (November 25, 1983).

[38] Cf. Novak, "The Politics of John Paul II," *Commentary* 31 (December, 1979); George Graham and George Carey, *The Post-Behavioral Era* (New York: David McKay, 1972); James Gould and Vincent Thursby, *Contemporary Political Thought* (New York: Holt, Rinehart & Winston, 1969).

[39] Edmund Burke, *Reflections on the Revolution in France* (Chicago: Gateway, 1955), p. 24.

[40] Reinhold Niebuhr, in *Perspectives on Political Philosophy* (1953; reprint ed., New York: Holt, Rinehart & Winston, 1971), 1:243-57.

[41] Cf. Schall, "Political Theory and Political Theology," *Laval Théologique et Philosophique* 31 (février, 1975).

[42] Cf. Frederick Wilhelmsen, *Christianity and Political Philosophy* (Athens: University of Georgia Press, 1978); Harry Jaffa, *Thomism and*

Aristotelianism (1952; reprint ed., Westport, Conn.: Greenwood Press, 1979).

[43] Cf. Jacques Maritain, *The Social and Political Philosophy of Jacques Maritain* (1955; reprint ed., South Bend, Ind.: University of Notre Dame Press, 1973); Josef Pieper, *The Silence of St. Thomas* (Chicago: Logos, 1957); Schumacher, *op. cit.*

[44] G.K. Chesterton, *The Well and the Shallows* (New York: Sheed and Ward, 1937), p. 82.

[45] Cf. Etienne Gilson, *Reason and Revelation in the Middle Ages* (1937; reprint ed., New York: Scribner's, 1966); Pieper, *Scholasticism* and *Silence;* Maurice de Wulf, *Philosophy and Civilization in the Middle Ages* (1922; reprint ed., New York: Dover, 1953); Charles Morris Cochrane, *Christianity and Classical Culture* (1940; reprint ed., New York: Oxford University Press, 1977); Christopher Dawson, *Religion and the Rise of Western Culture* (Garden City: Doubleday Image, 1958); Gilbert Meilaender, *The Taste for the Other: The Social and Ethical Ideas of C.S. Lewis* (Grand Rapids, Mich.: Eerdmans, 1978); McCoy, *op. cit.;* John Senior, *The Death of Christian Culture* (New Rochelle, N.Y.: Arlington House, 1978); Schall, *The Distinctiveness of Christianity* (San Francisco: Ignatius Press, 1983).

[46] Cf. Schall, "The Old Testament and Political Theory," *The Homiletic and Pastoral Review* 80 (November, 1979).

[47] Cf. Schall, "The Death of Christ and Political Theory," *Worldview* (March, 1978); "Political Philosophy and Christian Intelligence," *Catholicism-in-Crisis* 2 (November, 1983). "The Death of Christ" and "The Old Testament and Political Theory" (see above, note 46) will appear in Schall, *The Politics of Heaven and Hell: Christian Themes from Classical, Medieval, and Modern Political Philosophy* (Washington: University Press of America, 1984).

The Things of Caesar:
Toward the Delimitation
of Politics

Claes Ryn

MUCH CURRENTLY FASHIONABLE political theory has a pronounced reductionistic tendency. Human nature is pressed into schemes of explanation which fail to do justice to the complexity and richness of life. To give a few examples, the Marxists would have us treat human motives solely in terms of economics, the Freudians in terms of sexuality, and those in the tradition of Machiavelli and Hobbes in terms of the self-centered pursuit of power. It can be argued that these themes emerge, not from an openness to all aspects of experience, but from a selective and undue concentration on particular elements of life which are also prematurely defined. Political and social thought needs to broaden and deepen the context within which it contemplates its subject-matter, partly by reacquainting itself with dimensions of experience which have received little attention in this century. We can hope to approach the nature of politics with a measure of proportion and balance only if we can honestly say that no permanent aspect of life to which it is related has been ignored or denied study on its own terms. Only then are we likely to be able to define the scope of politics and know in general what to expect and not to expect from it.

I shall argue that our understanding of politics can be advanced by reconsidering and developing an old distinction which was once prominent in Western thought but is often ignored today – that between the things of God and the things of Caesar. I am intimating that an adequate theory of politics may have to incorporate in some form a grasp of the divine. This is not to suggest that the political theorist must become a theologian or embrace a particular religious creed, but that he be willing to examine on its own ground the general quality of life which has given rise to such concepts as "the holy," "the sacred,"or "the divine." That does not require going outside of human experience, only attending to its full range. The things of God and their relation to politics can be pursued as a *philosophical* problem, that is, without reliance on religious dogma.

A closely related step toward the proper delimitation of politics is to develop another distinction, one between the things of Caesar and those humanistic intellectual-artistic activities (either conceptual or aesthetical) which can be symbolized as the things of Apollo. Not only is the primary responsibility of the politician different from that of the priest, but it is different from that of the scholar and the artist. Although men may be obligated to the same ultimate moral goal, they must serve it in different ways as they have different abilities and opportunities. To the extent that a person wants to achieve truth or beauty, he must respect the standards intrinsic to these pursuits. And they demand first of all something other than practical prudence, which is the primary responsibility of the statesman. The task of philosophy is to give a truthful account of these various activities and their relationships to each other, including the role of philosophy itself in the larger whole.

II

IT MAY BE HELPFUL to make explicit a principle of logic which I associate with all philosophical investigations. Philosophy attempts to bring the totality of human experience to bear on each particular subject. Whatever it contemplates is thus understood in its relation to everything else. Taking politics as an example, we can be said truly to know it only insofar as we also know what it is not. But if philosophy aims to see the particular as a part of the whole, it does not grow in insight by some process of mere addition. The kind of comprehensiveness it seeks is a grasp of the *categorial structure* of experience. Philosophy looks for the permanent *forms* of human activity which contain within their qualitative polarity the infinite multiplicity of individual events.[1] Finding the universal structure of existence is not a matter of collecting and classifying "data" in a positivistic or pragmatic manner. Philosophical insight is creative and discriminating in a higher sense. It is a cognitive process in which man's historical experience is ordered by an immediate perception of the transcendent categories of reality and in which that same organizing awareness emerges out of the material of the past. This conceptual grasp of life is at once synthetical and analytical. In philosophical reflection, the human spirit recognizes itself, as it were, in its historical manifestations. In his finest achievements, his most illustrious science, his most elevated art and literature, his most noble laws, his highest religion, and in his corresponding retrogressions, man discovers the enduring forms of his humanity and their respective opposing potentialities. The true nature of phenomena is revealed in proportion as such comprehensiveness is achieved.[2] From the adequate vantage point, it is possible to understand the partial validity or lack of validity of less comprehensive points of view. The philosophical concept incorporates in itself their element of truth. From the inadequate point of view, it is only possible to understand your own position and those which are even less inclusive. To the intellectual philistine the insights of true philosophy will seem unintelligible (or perhaps so simple-minded as to raise doubts about the competence of the philosopher).

To illustrate, the "aristocratic" philosopher in Plato's *Republic* has no difficulty understanding the undisciplined pursuit of pleasure which Plato calls "democratic." This is because the "democratic" inclination is a dimension or moment in the life of all men. Indeed, the point is that "aristocratic man" has a better understanding of this state of character than does "democratic man" himself, for the former can relate it not just to what is below it but to what is above it. The nature of the "aristocratic" state is known precisely in its relation of superiority to other dimensions of the human. "Democratic man," on the other hand, can have little or no grasp of the philosophical insight and happiness which is inherent in "aristocratic" character, for he is looking in from the outside, or, perhaps more appropriately put, looking up from below. His understanding is limited by his merely partial, egocentrical experience of life. This may not stop him from making pronouncements about life in general and about "aristocratic man" in particular. But, regardless of their emotional intensity, his words carry little weight, for he is judging the higher by the lower. He is forcing into the perspective of his own limited awareness of life a reality which is immeasurably richer. Using this example, I am of course assuming that Plato's moral and intellectual vantage point approaches the kind of comprehensiveness which is the goal of philosophy.[3]

The same basic principle of logic can be illustrated in an analysis of the common modern belief, stemming from Machiavelli and Hobbes, that politics is simply a war of ego against ego. According to this view, peace and law are themselves only an enlightened manner of conducting the perpetual conflict. And it may well be asked if any realistic thinker could deny the element of truth in this theory. It certainly has greater plausibility than any statement to the opposite effect. But how could we claim really to know the nature and role of egotistical self-interest without also somehow knowing about a quality of life which is contrary to it and in relation to which selfishness can be recognized as such? Those who put all of their emphasis on egotism cannot help but give implicit recognition to that other dimension, but they do not explore it on its own ground and are thus left with a one-sided conception of existence. Philosophical comprehensiveness demands that the context be restored. Selfishness must be consciously related to its moral opposite, including man's experience of the divine.

A similar lack of compensatory balance is exhibited by many today who do talk a great deal about the need for morality in politics. There are those, for example, who retain some of the traditional religious beliefs, if only in name, but who are drawing from the modern secular mind a highly optimistic notion of what can be accomplished by political means. To them, the old idea that politics at its very best can be found somewhere between divine perfection and gross selfishness would seem too unassuming. The ambitious mission of politics must be to establish the rule of love and brotherhood as understood in the teachings of Christ. The Sermon on the Mount and other expressions of the summit of religious aspiration should become the basis for a political program. The result is to invest politics with divine potential. The true believer should become God's politician. This tendency is exemplified by pacifism, viewed at the same time as a political and a religious doctrine. Turning the other cheek should be regarded as also a prescription for politics. Blessed are the peacemakers. Another example is religious socialism which demands a transformation of society in what is taken to be the Christian spirit of sharing and brotherhood. One kind of one-sidedness that may be criticized in these cases is that the politicians of God are not sufficiently sensitive to the nature of man as we know it in actual political experience. In their emphasis on the obligation of bringing the things of God into the world of government, they tend toward utopian wishful thinking. And just as the cynical Machiavellian may be accused of distorting the nature of politics because of insufficient attention to what transcends conflict, so the politicians of God may be criticized for misconstruing the divine partly because of an inadequate grasp of the inescapable, grimmer aspects of politics. Thus, those who would put politics in the service of divine ends could be aided toward a clearer understanding of the kingdom of God by learning a few things from Machiavelli. One's knowledge of something is enhanced by seeing what it is not. We may speak of philosophical insight as the dialectical perception of complementary truths.

III

TRYING TO DELIMIT the sphere of the political, one has to survey a wealth of historical material fraught with extraordinary complexity. The history of the institutions of Church and State offers no sure guide to the categorial structure of human experience, although the development of these institutions may be viewed as examples of man groping his way toward giving each permanent aspect of life its due. I shall try to make the distinction between the things of God and the things of Caesar sufficiently clear to demonstrate its significance for the proposed reorientation of political thought. This requires that I touch also upon a closely related problem, that of distinguishing between the things of God and Caesar, respectively, and the things of Apollo. If Apollo, like Caesar, is *ultimately* a servant of morality and even religion, the terms upon which that service is rendered are *sui generis*.

A brief and very selective historical survey, for the limited purpose of giving some concreteness to the primary distinction I am pursuing, may concentrate on the West and start with Plato.[4] One finds in that philosopher a revealing tension. In *The Republic*, Plato is concerned, on the one hand, with raising politics to the ideal of transcendent perfection. Although the rulers of his city are not exactly priests and although he does not associate the eternal with a personal deity, it is possible to describe his ideal of government as

theocentric or theocratic. The philosopher rulers are supposed to
be singularly devoted to the Universal Good. There are even some
striking parallels between the communal life prescribed for them
and that of members of religious orders, as we know them in Christianity, for instance. But Plato's tendency to merge government
and religion is balanced by an opposite tendency. He also has a
strong sense that no identification between the political and the
divine is possible, even in the unlikely event that the most favorable
circumstances would be present. He leaves us with a curious
paradox. He points out that those who have risen to the culmination of philosophy will be so overwhelmed by the presence of the
Good that they will really prefer to devote all of their time to its
contemplation. "It won't be surprising if those who get so far are
unwilling to involve themselves in human affairs."[5] Plato is suggesting that the momentum which is intrinsic to the spiritual-
intellectual life tends to reduce man's attachment to this world, to
detach him, specifically, from politics. In this regard, too, Plato, for
all of his intellectualism, is similar to founders of religious orders
who have seen "otherworldliness" as the apex of the spiritual life.
What really matters to the *religiosi* is not the political kingdom,
but the kingdom of God. To explain how the philosophers can be expected to return into the cave to serve the cause of political justice,
Plato simply refers to necessity: only if these men are willing to
govern, can the degrading alternative of rule by unworthy men be
avoided.

There is, then, for Plato something about political life which
makes it resistant to and perhaps, in the end, radically incompatible with, the maintenance of the most pure orientation of the soul.
By its very nature, the obligation which drags the philosopher
down into the darkness of the cave is inhibiting his absorption in
transcendent perfection. Plato does not resolve this paradox. He
comes close to but does not break through to a distinction between
divine things and political things. And it may be argued that
because of this failure he is led both to exaggerate the moral potential of politics, which is given a quasi-divine mission, and to
underestimate the nature and scope of the Good.

Turning briefly to Plato's most illustrious student, we note that
for Aristotle, too, politics is understood as serving properly a
universal moral standard. But in relation to Plato's *Republic*, the
expectations placed on politics have been considerably reduced.

Significantly, Aristotle's realistic adjustments to the imperfections of this life are coupled with the beginnings of the kind of distinction I am trying to develop. In the notion of a contemplative life set apart from ordinary citizenship, he is on his way to the discovery that the fullest possible commitment to the divine requires or carries with it a certain removal from political concerns. Referring to the special happiness which belongs to the man who realizes the contemplative idea, Aristotle observes that "it is not insofar as he is man that he will live so, but insofar as something divine is present in him."[6] The divine tends to pull man out of the kind of life which is practiced by the good citizen. The most perfect type of happiness requires very little in the way of worldly amenities.

It should be added that despite the similarities between this idea and the idea of saintliness in the higher religions, Aristotle's contemplative life, like its counterpart in Plato, has a marked intellectualistic slant. His notion of otherworldliness would appear to incorporate to a large extent the kind of detachment which can be found in the true philosopher-scholar. We may perhaps speak, therefore, of a propensity in Aristotle to merge the things of God with the things of Apollo, meaning by the latter symbol those aspects of the effort to develop life's higher potential which are predominantly theoretical (philosophical or aesthetical).

Christianity offers a plethora of material pointing toward a sharpening of the primary distinction I am pursuing. We have it on the highest authority that we should render unto Caesar the things that are Caesar's and unto God the things that are God's.[7] Coupled with many of Christ's other statements, such as "my kingdom is not of this world,"[8] this admonition leaves little doubt that identification of the divine and the political is ruled out.

The central issue may be brought out by considering the encounter between Christ and the rich young man who has lived in accordance with the law and wants to know what he should do to inherit eternal life. We learn that Christ has the highest regard for this man, who is apparently a truly noble individual. According to St. Mark, Christ "loved him."[9] We remind ourselves that Christ does not conceive of his own mission as revoking the law. Those who are able to live according to the Commandments in the manner of the young man are far advanced in the spiritual life. But this life is not the highest possible kind. It may be good conduct and sufficient, as Christ allows, to "enter into life,"[10] but it is not saintliness.

In response to the young man's statement that he has already observed the Commandments for many years, Christ offers him the vision of otherworldliness: "If thou wilt be perfect," give away what you have and "follow me."[11] We may interpret this to mean that the young man is invited to go beyond the kind of life he has attained. The person who feels called to become literally like Christ would leave behind normal worldly concerns, and not least material belongings, as the disciples had done.[12] Nothing should stand in the way of the culmination of love. We may guess that, understanding this, the rich young man comes to see that this most demanding form of religious devotion is not for him. Turning away, he does not abandon his former spiritual commitment. But he now understands the law and his own role better. His may be an admirable kind of life, but there is an even higher order of religious aspiration. Presumably, the young man continues to seek the type of perfection which is compatible with ordinary social life, *e.g.,* family responsibilities, participation in politics, business enterprise, and military service. But he can be expected to do so with a new sense of humility and proportion. If the young man had made the choice that was made by Christ's disciples, he would have turned in a different direction. He would have adopted *for himself* the goal of holiness. This ideal is expressed, for instance, in the Sermon on the Mount, whose spirit can be summed up in these words: "Be ye therefore perfect, even as your Father which is in heaven is perfect."[13] *This* kind of perfection might indeed entail turning the other cheek, walking the extra mile, sharing everything, and taking no thought for the morrow. The individual who is trying to live now as in the kingdom of God is trying to sever all but the necessary ties to this world. Christ asks his disciples, "When I sent you without purse, and scrip, and shoes, lacked ye any thing?" And they reply, "Nothing."[14]

In the East, a very similar religious ideal is found in Buddhism. To take just a few examples out of the *Dhammapada,* which is attributed to the Buddha himself, the Brahman "has cut all fetters"; he is "free from all and every bondage"; he "calls nothing his own." Embodying the spirit of non-violence, he does not "let himself fly at his aggressor," and he "does not kill nor cause slaughter."[15]

Fully aware that we are moving across extremely difficult ground, I venture the suggestion that these religious ideals should not be viewed as prescribing for ordinary social and political life.

They reveal to all, but lead only some few to try actually to attain, a life of holiness. This special kind of witnessing to the kingdom of God involves the individual's detachment in some form from normal human concerns. That separation is both symptom and prerequisite of the most unqualified kind of attachment to God and indirectly to man. Genuinely religious otherworldliness, as I understand it, is not an escape from this world in the sense of a flight from burdensome duties to self and others. On the contrary, it demands even more than the high responsibilities assumed by the rich young man. But this calling is manifested as a release from what is unnecessary to, or standing in the way of, the culmination of love. The love of the holy man knows no bounds. It extends beyond family, friends, associates and nation. He is attaining to a loving identification with mankind. This spiritual disposition should not be confused with the merely sentimental mode of caring for humanity common in modern Western society. The love of the saintly person is the result of a more than merely human exertion of the will, whereas the most prevalent modern kind of caring for the world's unfortunate would appear to have few, if any, prerequisites in the way of personal moral self-improvement.[16]

Christ's explicit sanctioning of the role of Caesar is clear evidence that he regards political government as necessary to man's welfare in this world, perhaps also indirectly to the fulfillment of man's ultimate destiny. St. Paul goes very far when he insists that every soul "should be subject unto the higher powers. For there is no power but of God: the powers that be are ordained of God."[17] It is implied that it is possible, at least for most men and in normal circumstances, to be loyal to Caesar while serving God.

It is appropriate here to turn to the doctrine of the two swords, which has exerted a considerable influence on thinking about the proper relationship between Church and State in the Western world. We find in that doctrine, related to the teaching of St. Augustine, a belief that two types of authority are needed to save man from selfishness and hedonism. The Church keeps man ever mindful of the kingdom of God, and the State gives at least indirect support to the same ultimate goal by giving the proper direction to temporal existence, providing among other things the kind of social environment in which the Church can do its work. The two swords are ideally mutually supportive, and yet they are wielded independently in their own sphere. In a famous letter to the emperor,

Pope Gelasius I points out that both spheres of authority are from God. They are both needed to carry out the plan of creation. In another place, Gelasius argues that God "separated the kingly duties and powers from the priestly, according to different functions and dignity proper to each." This was done "to the end that spiritual employment might be removed from carnal diversions and that the soldier of the Lord might be as little as possible entangled in secular business, and that one involved in secular affairs might not be occupying the leadership of the Church. Thus it was sought to secure that both the orders might be humble since no man could combine eminence in both of them, and that the profession of each might be suited to the special aptitudes of those who follow it."[18] Gelasius's theory does not attempt to define for all times what are the boundaries in practice of each type of authority, but it is quite clear that politics is viewed as placing very different requirements on the men of the state than does the kingdom of God on the pope and the priests. There must always be a tension between full devotion to the things of God and the proper attention to worldly government. The emperor should always be mindful of what lies beyond politics and what is required for his own salvation, but he also has a special responsibility for the well-being of society, which sets him apart from the priests.

St. Augustine senses more strongly than most the awesome, compelling presence of the divine kingdom and its distance from ordinary life in this world. For all the complexities and varying emphases of his thought, its general tendency is reflected in his words, "I care to know only God and the soul, and nothing more."[19] In his distinction between the City of God and the Earthly City, which do not necessarily correspond to the visible institutions of Church and State, he may be criticized for a lack of balance and proportion. According to St. Augustine, every person belongs to either of the two cities – which one depends on the love which inspires him. Love of God makes the individual a citizen of the City of God, whereas love of self, meaning selfish love, assigns the individual to the Earthly City, the city of eternal punishment. What St. Augustine has to say about those who are elected to eternal happiness is not unambiguous, but his references to a community of saints would seem to suggest that he associates their characters with the virtue of otherworldliness in some sense of that word. Those who do not love in this manner are members of the Earthly City.[20] Where does that place the good man of Plato or Aristotle? It would be highly questionable to describe him as inspired by selfish love. On the contrary, his life is marked by the effort to rise out of egoism to love of the universal Good. Still, there appears to be no room in St. Augustine's scheme for this man. St. Augustine recognizes only a saint-like devotion to God, and its opposite, love of the selfish ego. The idea of a special type of worldly existence which is valuable in itself is not considered. According to Etienne Gilson, "such an idea seems never to have occurred to St. Augustine."[21] So overwhelmed is the latter by the perfection and the demands of the kingdom of God that, by contrast, temporal existence is reduced in the direction of futility. Concentration on the vision of otherworldliness leads in St. Augustine to a partial neglect of the potentialities of this life and, most importantly, of its potential for a moral refinement and happiness of its own. Government becomes for him little more than a remedy for sin. It should be noted that the element of one-sidedness in St. Augustine points in the opposite direction of the ideas of the modern politicians of God. Discounting almost completely the moral capacity of politics, he lends even less support to expectations that the things of God might become also the things of Caesar.

Being, among other things, one of those to introduce Aristotelian themes into Western Europe, St. Thomas Aquinas helps to restore some dignity to life in this world as a good in itself. In the idea of natural law, for example, he gives recognition to the possibility of temporal perfection apart from divine revelation. He also has a doctrine of two ways to salvation, one good and the other better. He makes a distinction between two ways of loving God, forming levels within the ascent toward Christian charity. The first and most commonly attainable kind of devotion is within the reach of those who are living ordinary social lives, attending to various worldly matters. The second type is for those few who are able to take the most direct route to the kingdom of God, avoiding hindrances. Both orientations are needed. The *religiosi* and those who perform worldly functions each serve God by aiming for the type of perfection which is compatible with their respective calling.[22] Aquinas recognizes the ideal of holiness, but without depreciating the values of a less exalted human existence. He remains aware of the difference and possible tension between the kingdom of God and the kingdom of Caesar. "In order that spiritual things might be distinct from earthly things, the ministry of that government was not committed to earthly kings but to priests."[23]

In succeeding centuries, which see a further reaction against a perceived failure to give this life its due in the medieval period, there are numerous examples of renewed attention to values of a more worldly type also among those who remain committed to Christianity. In Dante, for instance, we find a strong emphasis on the higher possibilities inherent in temporal existence. His humanistic bent is coupled with an explicit distinction between things divine and things political.

> Twofold . . . are the ends which unerring Providence has ordained for man: the bliss of this life, which consists in the functioning of his own powers, and which is typified by the earthly paradise; and the bliss of eternal life, which consists in the enjoyment of that divine vision to which he cannot attain by his own powers, except they be aided by the divine light, and this state is made intelligible by the celestial Paradise. These two states of bliss, like two different goals, man must reach by different ways. For we come to the first as we follow the philosophical teachings, applying them according to our moral and intellectual capacities; and we come to the second as we follow the spiritual teachings which transcend human reason according to our theological capacities, faith, hope, and charity.[24]

The "supreme pontiff" guides mankind to "life eternal," and the emperor guides them to "temporal happiness." It might be observed in passing that the things of Apollo here tend to merge with the things of Caesar.

Paradoxically, the tension between the divine and the political has been recognized in various ways also by leading Western thinkers who are departing from the religious traditions of their society. Machiavelli and Rousseau are two cases in point. Machiavelli directs against historical Christianity the charge that it did not equip men for this world, and particularly not for the rough world of politics. Meekness and other Christian virtues are not adequate for that sphere of activity.[25] It may be argued against Machiavelli that he is misunderstanding Christianity and judging it on the basis of limited historical evidence. He seems to associate the Christian attitude toward politics with the saintly virtues, faulting it for turning the other cheek to those who would destroy the state. But this Machiavellian interpretation, questionable though it be, is illuminating. In his own way, Machiavelli senses the tension between otherworldliness, which is an element in all genuine religion, and the requirements of politics. In the *Social Contract*, Rousseau is seeking to provide for unquestioning loyalty to the political sovereign. He rightly views Christianity as posing a serious threat to that kind of citizenship. He writes: "Christianity is a wholly spiritual religion, concerned solely with the things of heaven; the Christian's homeland is not of this world." The true Christian exhibits, Rousseau believes, a "profound indifference" to the things of this world, which is hardly a desirable trait in a citizen of the state. Like Machiavelli, Rousseau associates what he takes to be the genuinely Christian attitude toward politics with the saintly virtues. This is why it seems to him that "a society of true Christians would not be a society of men."[26] Machiavelli and Rousseau are thus in a way quite alert to something about Christianity which runs counter to the tendency of interpretation among the modern politicians of God, namely, that it directs the attention of the most devoted men of religion away from worldly affairs and particularly politics.

In anticipation of an argument to follow, we may end this brief survey by singling out the issue of war. Overwhelming evidence suggests that the idea of pacifism, viewed as a doctrine binding on all, is alien to the mainstream of the Christian tradition. Even St. Augustine has a doctrine of the just war. To be sure, war-making and other kinds of violence have generally been considered incompatible with the life of the representatives of the kingdom of God, that is, priests and the religious of different types. For others, however, war-making may be a moral duty in certain circumstances. The Orient offers examples of a similar view. The Hindu religion regards it as a sin for a Brahman to fight – he serves the ideal of non-resistance – but the *Ksatriyas*, the nobility and warrior caste, have the duty of fighting for a righteous cause when no alternative is available.[27] In a world of selfish ambition, arbitrariness, greed, stubbornness, and pride, violence is sometimes necessary to protect or secure justice.

It seems to me difficult to avoid the conclusion that the more than merely human devotion to perfection that one finds in some of the most ardent followers of Christ, or of Buddha in the East, does not belong to the same level of aspiration as worldly civilization, although the latter could be viewed as serving the divine indirectly.

The distinction which is emerging may be summed up in the following tentative way: Within the moral life there may be discerned two orders of perfection. There exist among men rare individuals whose central inspiration is the specifically religious vision of holiness. They are in a sense beyond the political commonwealth. And there are those, far more common and yet none too numerous, who aspire to the kind of moral virtue which is appropriate to ordinary human life.[28] As models for actual adoption, these two types of life must diverge. But they are also intimately related in that they serve in different ways the fulfillment of human existence. Both are morally ennobling dispositions. The end of politics falls far short of the most demanding religious ideal, but it is still an obligation to rise above the clash of selfish wills. It should be understood that the two lifestyles are conceived in this discussion, not as objectives already attained, but as general orientations within which very different stages of development are possible. In some individuals the two may perhaps actually coexist for a time in uneasy balance. Yet, even though one should not identify philosophical categories of activity with particular individuals, I am suggesting that the sense of direction intrinsic to each orientation is monopolistic in the sense that it cannot become fully realized in practice without excluding the other.

I would argue, then, that although all men are morally obligated to try to perfect themselves, those who are assuming responsibility for our welfare in human society should try to realize, not saintliness, but the *counterpart* of the specifically religious striving which is appropriate to their calling. We may term this virtue righteousness. Emphasizing what separates the two orders of aspiration rather than what they have in common, the more worldly type of moral discipline could also be called the pursuit of justice or civilization. The righteous individual is trying to make the best of this world, in a transcendent meaning of the word "best." He seeks to promote this life's potential for goodness, and for truth, beauty, and economic well-being as means to moral perfection. It should be pointed out that this kind of orientation, as I understand it, does not exclude, but is perfectly compatible with, what is usually meant by religion. Individuals of this type who are also Christians are of course trying to serve God in their particular lives and occupations, but they have chosen as *their* primary responsibility the effort to elevate temporal existence in the direction of its own intended perfection. Those who would be righteous are not, like the *religiosi,* turning away from this world, but trying to realize its higher values. To take an example from politics, it is not expected of the statesman that he should take no thought for the morrow or turn the other cheek in the conduct of his duties. That might jeopardize the very existence of the civilized order of which he is a trustee. On the contrary, civilization needs to plan for its own material well-being as a means to its higher ends, and it needs to protect itself against those who would threaten its values by force. At the same time, the person who is aiming at the "worldly" counterpart of saintliness shares with him who is trying to be literally like Christ some of his lightheartedness in regard to this world. The truly civilized individual is not obsessed with personal power, material comfort or even life itself. He is attempting to put them in the service of man's moral end. In some circumstances he would even be willing to part with them. It is life of a certain quality, not mere existence, which has value.

It may be suggested that the civilized orientation is strengthened by awareness of the saintly values. The latter exert a moral pull which helps to keep worldly existence from deteriorating into a pursuit of hedonistic or utilitarian gratification. The vision of holiness is shared by the civilized man, although from a distance, and is in that sense supportive of the transcendent standard inherent in the civilizing effort itself. Conversely, human society, when living up to its higher mission, can offer support for values belonging to the kingdom of God. In a society where not even the moral discipline of righteousness is attempted, the more demanding ideal of holiness is not likely to be understood, much less emulated. But where genuine civilization is strong, the specifically religious values can thrive in a congenial atmosphere. In such a society, an individual who is following the goal of otherworldliness may actually be able to practice virtues like non-violence with a degree of personal safety. We can perhaps speak, then, of the virtues of righteousness and holiness as existing in a state of creative and enriching tension.

One effect of this thesis about two kinds of moral aspiration is to divorce politics, except as indicated, from the goals of divine perfection. Recognizing that the latter cannot be achieved by political means, politics is held up to a much less strict, but still highly demanding moral standard. Achieving even such elementary prerequisites of civilized existence as law and order is a very difficult task, indeed, beyond the capacity of many societies. And if we may associate civilization roughly with Aristotle's idea of the good life, it is clear that its realization is quite a remarkable achievement in itself.

But here an important complication, which has only been hinted at so far, should be brought into the open. Caesar has been used as the symbol for the attempt to promote and coordinate the aspirations of human society through politics. However, it needs to be stressed that even when understood in the highest and widest possible sense, politics is but one aspect of the civilizing effort. The latter is advanced in decisive ways by all of those social activities whose primary purpose is not practical but theoretical. These activities reach their highest intensity in poets, artists, philosophers, and the like. Such men serve values without which no genuine civilization can be imagined, namely, truth and beauty (and the moral good through these). Individuals who cultivate the human spirit in this way may be described as having charge of the things of Apollo. As participants in the effort to enrich worldly existence, they are "humanistic" in orientation. In favorable circumstances it is sometimes possible for these servants of Apollo to join forces with the servants of Caesar in the cause of civilization. But the "righteousness" appropriate to their high calling should still be distinguished from that of the statesman. Their work has its special values and demands. Indeed, the intellectual-artistic life is pursued by some men with such dedication as to produce in them a kind of "otherworldliness" of its own. This is already recognized, although in a rather ambiguous way, in Plato's and Aristotle's conception of a contemplative existence. When pursued to the fullest, theoretical activity (whether conceptual or imaginative) tends to reduce a person's concern about some other things of this life such as political power or material comfort. But in spite of a certain surface resemblance, this type of "otherworldliness" should not be loosely identified with the specifically religious aspiration already described. Also when philosophy or art seek to articulate the quality of experience here called holiness, the mode of experience is theoretical and not practical. Insofar as theoretical pursuits are a wish to enrich life with truth and beauty for their own sake, they are a part of worldly civilization. At the same time, it should be carefully observed that this humanistic discipline contains the potential for serious conflict with Caesar. The requirements of politics are sometimes incompatible with the needs and responsibilities of the intellectual-artistic life. For example, if in some difficult circumstances the truth should become a threat to the very survival of political order, not even the most noble statesman may have any choice but to turn against it. The intellectual-artistic pursuits, for their part, betray their highest nature if they allow themselves to be swayed by or enlisted in the support of particular political causes.[29] It would appear, therefore, that to the distinction between the things of God and the things of Caesar should be added distinctions between both of these and the things of Apollo.

It may be well to underscore that the dimensions of life here symbolized as separate "things" are understood as universal forms of human activity and in that sense as present in every individual. They are potentialities, more or less developed in particular persons, which together constitute our humanity. Thus, to say about a poet, for instance, that he is the servant of Apollo is not to deny that he also participates in other aspects of experience. The symbol draws attention to the special emphasis of his life through which he contributes to the larger perfection of existence. In that perfection the categories of human activity tend to coalesce without losing their separate identities. It is freely granted that concern about truth and beauty may be subordinate parts of both a political and a saintly aspiration.

Perhaps it also needs to be made explicit that while the theoretical life is set apart from the specifically religious and political spheres by the nature of the obligation intrinsic to it, it does of course also encompass these other spheres (and itself) in its own philosophical or aesthetical *contemplation* of life's different aspects. The interpretation here offered is one example of an attempt to achieve conceptual comprehensiveness. But, as such, this attempt is judged not by its moral goodness but by its degree of truth.

IV

THOSE WHO ARGUE for close correspondence or identity between the highest religious ideals and political ideals – the religious pacifists, the religious socialists and the liberation theologians are contemporary examples – thereby show themselves to be ignoring or at least playing down very considerably the notion of holiness which is a central source of inspiration, not just in Christianity, but in Buddhism and other religions. To reject the vision of other-worldliness outright would be to sever openly the connection with all of the traditional higher religions. Instead, the politicians of God attempt to bring this ideal down into the political realm. But if my analysis is correct, this amounts to the same thing. To reiterate my logical theme, *the deification of politics requires the politization, and hence the devaluation, of the divine.* Particularly striking examples of this can be taken from liberation theology. In the following endorsement of political activism, one looks in vain for any trace of the spirit of holiness:

> The commitment of militant Christians to liberation is not confined to rhetorical professions of principles or to new conceptual models for the conduct of theology. It finds its expression in everyday life: Dominican priests in Brazil offer sanctuary to urban guerrillas; Protestant missionaries in Uruguay actively support the Tupamaros; United States churches contribute funds to liberation groups in South Africa and Mozambique; priests issue ultimatums to their religious superiors urging them to return church-owned lands to Bolivian peasants or to reject government subsidies for their schools. Such activities openly accept all political risks: suppression, jail, torture, exile, even assassination.[30]

Giving politics a divine mission, some Christians in name become difficult to distinguish from some of those who have explicitly rejected traditional religion. The Marxist idea of a communistic society, for instance, can be seen as a secular-romantic transformation of the religious vision of the Christian tradition. The culmination of man's aspirations in a stateless, harmonious society is to be attained through a collective, *political* redemption of mankind. As Eric Voegelin has demonstrated, the modern intellectual and political movements which he calls "gnostic" give divine (but in practice, rather, diabolical) status to such immanent powers as "reason," "science," and "the people."[31] In the belief that the highest values of the kingdom of God can be realized on a large scale in human societies, many modern Christians would appear to have gone almost as far toward making that very term, the kingdom of God, unnecessary. Values which are viewed in my analysis as finding a manifestation only in rare individuals of exceptional spiritual purpose and self-discipline are regarded as capable of realization in egalitarian abundance through political, perhaps revolutionary, reform of the social exterior. This is in effect to deny the special quality of witnessing described above.

We may take political pacifism advanced under religious auspices as another example of the attempt to merge politics and religion. I have in mind no particular formal doctrine, but the general impulse which has found expression, for instance, in anti-war movements in this century. This pacifist disposition, often vaguely articulated, can be criticized first by calling into question the understanding of the nature of politics that it implies. Does not this kind of pacifist need to learn the Machiavellian lesson? Politics, Machiavelli argues, is predominantly conflict between selfish interests. This conflict is just barely concealed in the more successful societies by the rule of law. To recognize an element of truth in this observation is not to adopt Machiavelli's amoral premises. Indeed, it is possible to view Machiavelli's teaching as in one respect a part or outgrowth of the tradition against which he revolts. Would he have arrived at his "realistic" view of politics, had he not learnt from his civilization and Christianity in particular to look behind the facade of human conduct to the hidden motives? To be sure, he tears the Christian emphasis on sinfulness out of context and blows it out of proportion in his rather cynical theory of politics. But his observations are not incompatible with the older view of life. It is even possible to argue that in his loosely and inconclusively formulated distinction between public and private life, he is groping his way toward an important insight regarding politics which is only imperfectly stated in the older tradition. That is to say that from Machiavelli, placed in the proper context, the pacifist could learn a more realistic view of what to expect from politics.

If the pacifist can be criticized for uncritically running together the things of Caesar and the things of God, we may approach his confusion as symptomatic of two kinds of one-sidedness: exaggerating the moral potential of politics and underestimating the sacredness of the divine. Referring to the principle of the complementarity of insight, or, in this case, the compounding of error, the point would be that either distortion gives rise to the other. They are actually aspects of one and the same deficiency. If the highest values of religion are conceived as being within the reach of most men, then politics has become that much more appropriate to their attainment. And if politics is thus understood to have divine potential, the divine has been much reduced in the nature of its holiness.

To view certain sayings of Christ, such as the one about turning the other cheek, as being also political principles is the same as to ignore their status as expressions of a spiritual reality elevated even above man's noblest civilized achievements. This, I argue, represents a contraction of man's spiritual horizon. Are not those who find in the Sermon on the Mount the outlines for a political program insufficiently aware of the nature of the sacred? Their view of politics is symptomatic of not having discovered the spiritual life in its highest manifestation. An exaggerated notion of the moral potential of politics reveals a contracted and distorted awareness of the holy.

It is of course possible to question the appropriateness of some of the ways in which religious orders or individuals have attempted to embody the spirit of holiness. But it comes dangerously close to obscurantism not to take account in any form of the special quality of life to which Christ, and Buddha, and many of their followers have witnessed. Of the commitments through which particular individuals have sought to attach themselves completely to the divine, poverty, chastity, and non-violence are among the most demanding. Leaving aside the difficult question of the adequacy or necessity of these vows to the religious objective, my argument is that they cannot be held up as goals of politics. In the words of Walter Lippmann:

> Quite evidently the ideal of non-resistance would, if literally and consistently followed, abandon the world to the predatory. Poverty, universally practiced, would sink the world in squalor and darkness. Universal celibacy would extinguish human life. All this is so obvious that, manifestly, these ideas, which we find in all high religion, cannot be treated as public rules of human conduct. . . . They are the ideals of a realm of being where men are redeemed and regenerated and the evils of the world have been outgrown.

By its very nature, the aspiration toward holiness is not for everyone, except in the sense that, as Lippmann writes, it "sets before men a vision of themselves transformed."[32] If I am correct, this serves to encourage the counterpart of holiness which is within the reach of men who live ordinary lives – that is, righteousness.

Only if the political and civilizing order of perfection is recognized, can the specifically divine order be kept free from alien intrusions. Similarly, it is only if the religious ideal of otherworldliness is grasped in some way that the virtue of righteousness can be properly delimited. By the synthetical-analytical logic of complementarity, what can be learned from Machiavelli is at the same time a contribution toward a sharpening of our understanding of the divine.

V

TO LEARN THE MACHIAVELLIAN lesson is to discover that for Caesar to adopt the ideal of non-violence would be to unleash the unscrupulous. Pacifism, viewed as a political program, plays into the hands of the ruthless barbarian who is not impressed by sentimental appeals to love and brotherhood. An unrealistic assessment of what can be expected from people in politics may in some circumstances jeopardize the future of civilization, without which all higher values are lost. It might in fact be the height of immorality for a president of the United States, for example, to turn the other cheek in the conduct of foreign policy. He has promised those who elected him to preserve, protect, and defend the Constitution. He must take measures to deal with challenges as they appear, not in the dreams of wishful thinking, but in the real world. Anything else would be to betray his political trust. Obligated by the moral ideal of righteousness, he will of course seek ways to modify and soften the powerplay wherever possible. But he must do so in such a manner as to protect and promote the values of civilization, which is his primary responsibility. Making a telling point against religious-political pacifism, René de Visme Williamson observes that when Christ spoke of turning the other cheek he was addressing individuals, specifically the disciples, and not governments. "Jesus did not instruct his disciples to turn *other* people's cheeks, and governments are responsible for the welfare of peoples and not just themselves." Somebody who condones or encourages the burning of draft cards may, in Williamson's words, "become morally responsible for national disaster."[33]

Even if a person is deeply and genuinely religious, that does not in itself impart any knowledge about how moral values can be promoted in politics. It does not excuse anyone who would prescribe particular governmental measures from becoming first a master of the subject-matter. Speaking about those who have been outside the cave and seen the Good, Socrates points out that we should not "think it strange that anyone who descends from contemplation of the divine to human life and its ills should blunder and make a fool of himself . . . while still blinded and unaccustomed to the surrounding darkness."[34] A failure to acquire political prudence and knowledge may lead to endorsement of naive and ultimately destructive proposals. Assuming that a person actually possesses a morally pure intention, it is still important to heed Aristotle's admonition that "goodness in itself is not enough; there must also be the power to translate it into action."[35] It might be added that premature certainty about the proper means to an end is not just an intellectual but a moral failing. Indeed, a pure intention uninformed by knowledge of particular circumstances is highly suspect.

An individual with a more than superficial understanding of the nature of politics will be reluctant to commit God to any particular course of political action, except possibly in rare situations in which the facts are beyond all reasonable doubt. Politics is a sphere of activity where blinding passions, self-serving prejudice, arbitrariness, and other emotions force themselves on the participants. Given the nature of politics and that no man is omniscient or beyond moral weakness, judgments in this area which are completely free of vitiating influences are not normally to be expected. If, therefore, a priest implies that he is speaking for God when he advocates some political cause, he is running the risk of soiling the divine as well as the risk of violating his true mission. The step from concern about keeping man mindful of the divine to the propagation of political action is fraught with extreme moral danger.

As should be evident from my previous argument, these observations are not meant to suggest that religion and politics do not touch. Needless to say, an individual who knows, as a part of a civilized understanding of the purpose of life, about the nature of the divine will approach his own pursuits with a special seriousness because of it. Although my analysis creates a strong presumption that priests remove themselves, in their ministerial capacity at minimum, from direct involvement in political causes, there appears to be at least one way in which they can influence politics without violating their primary mission and risking to compromise their special standing and authority in the community. The priest does have a kind of expertise which can aid political decisions but which does not dictate particular solutions. He knows better than most the tendency of arbitrariness or premature certainty to cloud men's judgment, and he can offer instruction in how to identify and avoid them. By trying to make politicians and others aware of their egocentrical bias and seeking to restore their moral bearings, he makes the contribution to a sound accommodation of interests which is most appropriate to his own kind of authority. To the extent that he addresses political issues, his proper task is to purify the *spirit* in which decisions are made. Since politics is in its very essence the pursuit of influence by various groups, morality could not demand of the participants that they renounce partisanship in every sense of that word. Politics without partisanship would no longer be politics. It is not even a moral ideal, but an empty, unreal abstraction. Morality does not require of participating groups that they abandon every claim to attention for some allegedly disinterested blueprint of the good society. But they should let their demands be tempered by a concern for the good of other groups and of the whole. In this attempt to harmonize contending powers aimed at discovering what is legitimately due various groups, the priest can appeal to the moral conscience of those involved. He can inspire moral self-scrutiny through questions like these: "Are you truly convinced that your own party program is not just a blatantly partisan effort designed to gain advantages at the expense of other groups? Can you honestly say that you have considered the good of the whole? And have you minimized self-serving prejudice by taking in all of the relevant facts?" When it comes to actually formulating concrete political proposals, the priest yields humbly to others in awareness not just of the complexity of the issues but of his own primary function. He does not mandate a specific course of action, which would be to assume the role of servant to Caesar, but a certain *quality* of action.

In respect to worldly matters, the work of the priest can be said to run parallel to that of serious intellectuals and artists whose primary obligation is to Apollo. But whereas their first concern is to strengthen that in men which makes for a humane, civilized life, *his* ultimate purpose is to direct men's attention beyond even our highest worldly obligations. Thus, he serves neither Caesar nor Apollo.[36]

VI

THE PROPOSED DISTINCTION between the things of God and the things of Caesar brings into serious question various doctrines which would incorporate specifically religious ideals into politics. It invites a reassessment of both religion and politics, calling for a new sensitivity to the special character and requirements of each. To grasp the distinction is to become acutely aware of the moral limitations of politics and government. But this line of thinking is also a challenge to those who are inclined to deny the existence of a transcendent moral goal for politics. The distinction may counteract the questionable tendency in modern Western thought to view acceptance of such a higher end as dependent on acceptance of a theology. To the extent that inherited religious dogmas have been rejected in the West, intellectuals have felt compelled to abandon also the idea of a transcendent principle of good. This unfortunate situation is related in part to the inclination, particularly in traditional Protestant Christianity, to regard adoption of the Faith as a prerequisite for genuine morality. Man without the God of religious doctrine is man without transcendent moral standards – on this at least, atheistic intellectuals and many Christians would seem to agree. The suggested distinction makes politics primarily a non-religious concern. The things of Caesar are viewed as belonging to an order of activity whose highest moral aim is righteousness rather than divine perfection. It becomes possible, therefore, to consider the moral end of government without first committing oneself to a theology, although, as I have also argued, no philosophically comprehensive and proportionate treatment of politics appears possible without recognition of the divine as a universal category of human experience.

I am suggesting, in conclusion, that the political scientist can fully understand his own subject matter only in relation to what is not political. The distinction between the things of Caesar and the things of God, and between these and the things of Apollo, can be viewed as a step toward the type of comprehensiveness which is characteristic of philosophy. It helps to restore the totality to which politics belongs. A genuine understanding of the things of Caesar contains within itself an understanding of the things of God. That does not mean that the political thinker must be an authority on the divine as the theologian is an authority. What he needs is a philosophical grasp of the general quality or form of what has here been called the holy, the sacred, the saintly, the other-worldly, the divine. Similarly, no one truly knowledgeable in the divine things can be without a more than superficial grasp of political things, again in their general nature. The proposed distinction offers protection against both political utopianism and political cynicism. It counteracts simplistic and naive notions about the ability of government to transform the human condition. But it also directs attention to that moral potential which does belong to the sphere of politics. By relating our thinking to the great traditions, it has the additional benefit of liberating us from the bias of a narcissistic contemporaneousness.

Notes

¹ These categorial polarities, Benedetto Croce suggests, are good-evil, efficient-inefficient, true-false and beautiful-ugly. The first and the second, which pertain to practical willing, are treated in particular depth in his *Philosophy of the Practical: Economic and Ethic* (New York: Biblo and Tannen, 1967). (The translation is not without considerable flaws.) To Croce's categories may have to be added one that takes account of the special form of practical activity which will be referred to here as the potentiality of saintliness or otherworldliness. Croce's valid insights also have to be separated from his dubious monistic assumptions which deny the reality of evil.

² Contrary to the natural and experimental sciences, which have limited pragmatic objectives, and contrary to attempted imitations of their principles in other disciplines, *e.g.*, the social sciences, philosophy does not cut up reality into convenient manageable entities as a preliminary to studying it. Instead of tearing phenomena out of context and treating them in isolation as reified entities, it respects the living totality to which the object of study belongs. Philosophy alone is completely faithful to reality as we know it in immediate experience. The nature of philosophical logic is examined in Benedetto Croce, *Logica* (Bari: Laterza, 1967). (The English translation, *Logic as the Science of the Pure Concept* [London: Macmillan, 1917], is not entirely reliable.)

³ For Plato's discussion of the five states of the soul, see, in particular, *The

Republic VII-IX.

[4] Important historical material for an account of the emerging awareness in different cultures of the tension between the political and the divine is found in the works of Eric Voegelin. For some of the roots of the distinction between the things of God and the things of Caesar in Jewish culture, see *Israel and Revelation*, vol. 1 of *Order and History*, 4 vols. to date (Baton Rouge: Louisiana State University Press, 1956-74). The pre-Platonic awareness of two levels of higher aspiration is treated in *The World of the Polis*, vol. 2 of the same work, esp. pp. 111-241.

[5] Plato, *The Republic* VII. 517e, 2nd ed., rev. (Harmondsworth: Penguin Books, 1974), p. 321.

[6] Aristotle, *The Nicomachean Ethics* 1177b (London: Oxford University Press, 1966), p. 265.

[7] Luke 20:25.

[8] John 18:36.

[9] Mark 10:21.

[10] Matthew 19:21.

[11] *Ibid.*

[12] Although tenuous in some respects, the parallel should be noted between this religious vision and the belief of both Plato and Aristotle that ordinary family ties, material belongings, etc., are potentially unimportant and perhaps even hindrances to the highest kind of life.

[13] Matthew 5:48.

[14] Luke 22:35. Cf. Matthew 10:9-10.

[15] *The Dhammapada*, translated and with an essay by Irving Babbitt (New York: New Directions, 1965), pp. 58, 60, 61, 57, 59.

[16] Cf. Mark 10:29-30. See also P.E. More, *The Christ of the New Testament* (Princeton: Princeton University Press, 1924), chap. 7, and George Santayana, *Dominations and Powers* (New York: Charles Scribner's Sons, 1951), pp. 366-370.

[17] Romans 13:1.

[18] Quoted in Jerome G. Kerwin, *Catholic Viewpoint on Church and State* (Garden City: Hanover House, 1960), pp. 19-20.

[19] Quoted in Friedrich Heer, *The Intellectual History of Europe* (New York: The World Publishing Co., 1966), p. 21.

[20] See St. Augustine, *The City of God*, esp. XIV, chap. 28.

[21] Etienne Gilson, "Introduction," *The City of God* (Garden City: Image Books, 1958), p. 32.

[22] Cf. Heinrich Denifle, *Luther and Lutherdom* (Somerset, Ohio: Torch Press, 1917), vol. 1, chap. 8.

[23] St. Thomas Aquinas, *On Kingship* I. 14.

[24] Dante, *On World Government (De Monarchia)* (Indianapolis: Bobbs-Merrill, 1957), p. 78.

[25] See, for example, *The Discourses* II. 2.

[26] Jean-Jacques Rousseau, *The Social Contract* (Harmondsworth: Penguin Books, 1968), p. 183; 182 (bk. IV, chap. 8).

[27] See Sarvepali Radhakrishnan, *Eastern Religions and Western Thought* (London: Oxford University Press, 1939), esp. pp. 349-386.

[28] Although I do not claim to speak for any particular religious denomination, considerable support for my line of argument can be drawn from the traditions of Catholic Christianity, especially its distinctions between general duty and the way of the counsels and between the natural and the supernatural.

[29] For a discussion of the dangers to the world of thought from the passions of politics, see Julien Benda, *The Treason of the Intellectuals* (New York: Norton, 1969).

[30] Denis Goulet, *A New Moral Order: Studies in Development Ethics and Liberation Theology* (Maryknoll, N.Y.: Orbis Books, 1974), p. 84.

[31] Eric Voegelin, *From Enlightenment to Revolution,* ed. John Hallowell (Durham, N.C.: Duke University Press, 1976).

[32] Walter Lippmann, *The Public Philosophy* (New York: New American Library, 1955), p. 116.

[33] René de Visme Williamson, "The Institutional Church and Political Activity," *Modern Age* 18 (Spring, 1974): 166 (my emphasis).

[34] Plato, *The Republic* VII. 517d; p. 321.

[35] Aristotle, *Politics* VII (Harmondsworth: Penguin Books, 1962), p. 263.

[36] For an in-depth examination of the political implications of the ethical imperative in its civilizing rather than its specifically religious form, see my *Democracy and the Ethical Life: A Philosophy of Politics and Community* (Baton Rouge: Louisiana State University Press, 1978).

Notes on the Contributors

George W. Carey is Professor of Government at Georgetown University, where he teaches political theory. He is a member of the National Council on the Humanities and edits *The Political Science Reviewer*. Among Dr. Carey's writings are *Liberalism vs. Conservatism* co-edited with Willmoore Kendall, *Basic Symbols of the American Tradition* co-authored with Willmoore Kendall, and *A Second Federalist* with Charles S. Hyneman. His articles and reviews have appeared in *American Political Science Review*, *The Journal of Politics*, *Western Political Quarterly* and *Modern Age*.

Gerhart Niemeyer is Professor Emeritus of Government at the University of Notre Dame. He was a Fulbright Professor at the University of Munich, and Distinguished Visiting Professor at Hillsdale College, 1976-82. An ordained deacon of the Episcopal Church, Dr. Niemeyer is Vice-Chairman of the Board of Foreign Scholarships. He has served as a foreign service officer for the U.S. Department of State, is a past member of the Task Force on Foreign Policy of the Republican National Coordinating Committee, and is on the board of advisors of Young Americans for Freedom. His books include *Law Without Force, An Inquiry into the Soviet Mentality, The Communist Ideology, Between Nothingness and Paradise*, and *Deceitful Peace*.

Clifford Kossel, S.J. is Professor of Philosophy at Gonzaga University in Spokane, Washington. He is a member of the American Catholic Philosophical Association, past president of the Jesuit Philosophical Association, and is on the editorial board of *International Catholic Review: Communio*. Rev. Kossel has published articles in numerous periodicals, including *The Modern Schoolman, Jesuit Educational Quarterly*, the *Proceedings* of the Jesuit Philosophical Association, *Religious Education* and *Communio*, and in the *Encyclopedia of Morals* and *Readings in Ancient and Medieval Philosophy* (ed. James Collins).

Thomas Molnar is Professor of Philosophy and Humanities at the City University of New York. A member of the editorial board of *The Intercollegiate Review*, Dr. Molnar contributes frequently to scholarly journals and has authored 25 books, including *God and the Knowledge of Reality, The Decline of the Intellectual, Christian Humanism*, and *Politics and the State*.

Ellis Sandoz is Professor of Political Science at Louisiana State University in Baton Rouge. He is a member of the National Council on the Humanities, the Executive Council of the Southern Political Science Association, and is a former council member of the American Political Science Association. In addition to articles in academic journals, he has published three books: *Political Apocalypse: A Study of Dostoevsky's Grand Inquisitor*; *Conceived in Liberty: American Individual Rights Today*; and *The Voegelinian Revolution: A Biographical Introduction*. He has also edited *Eric Voegelin's Thought: A Critical Appraisal*, and is currently working on a collection of essays, *A Government of Laws: Essays on the American Founding*.

Paul Sigmund is Professor of Politics at Princeton University. A former National Endowment for the Humanities Fellow, he is a member of the American Political Science Association, the Latin American Studies Association, and Cusanus Gesellschaft. Dr. Sigmund is the author of six books, including *Nicholas of Cusa and Medieval Political Thought*, *Natural Law in Political Thought*, *The Overthrow of Allende and the Politics of Chile*, and, most recently, *Aquinas on Ethics and Politics*.

James V. Schall, S.J. is Associate Professor of Government at Georgetown University and was Consultor on the Pontifical Commission on Justice and Peace. Among his books are *Christianity and Politics*, *Redeeming the Time*, *Liberation Theology*, and, most recently, *The Politics of Heaven and Hell*. He has also published numerous essays in scholarly journals.

Claes Ryn is Chairman of the Department of Politics at the Catholic University of America. The recipient of fellowships from the Earhart Foundation and the Wilbur Foundation and a Richard M. Weaver Fellowship, Dr. Ryn is the author of *Democracy and the Ethical Life*, the forthcoming *Will, Imagination, and Reason* with Folke Leander, and a book on modern American intellectual and cultural conservatism published in Sweden. He has published in such journals as *Thought*, *Journal of Politics*, *Modern Age* and *The Political Science Reviewer*.

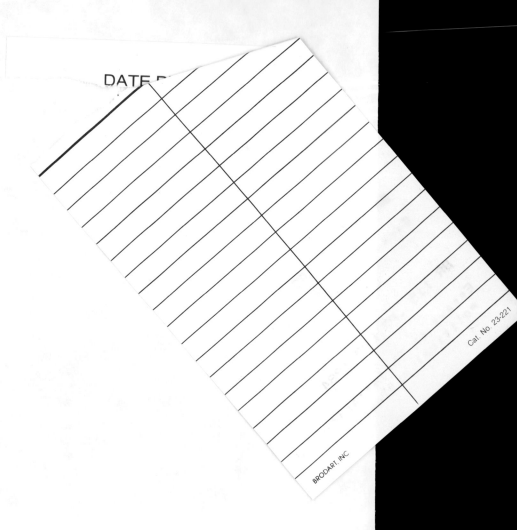